THE DECENTRALIST

MISSION, MORALITY, AND MEANING IN THE AGE OF CRYPTO

MAX BORDERS

EDITED BY
JAMES HARRIGAN

CONTENTS

Motivation: An Introduction

—

1. **Mission**: One Revolution
2. **Means**: Two Hands
3. **Minds**: Three Governors
4. **Matrix**: Four Forces
5. **Mutuality**: Five Disruptions
6. **Morality**: Six Spheres
7. **Mindfulness**: Seven Rituals
8. **Maturation**: Eight Stages
9. **Markets**: Nine Principles
10. **Meaning**: Ten Keys

—

Manichaeism: An Afterword
Mentions
Endnotes

Copyright © 2022 by Max Borders

ISBN 978-1-7320394-2-1

All rights reserved. No part of this book may be reproduced or transmitted in any form or by any means, electronic or mechanical, including photocopying, recording, or by any information storage and retrieval system, without written permission from the copyright owner.

For information on distribution rights, royalties, derivative words, or licensing opportunities on behalf of this content or work, please contact the publisher at the address below.

ORGANIZATIONS, INSTITUTIONS, AND INDUSTRY PUBLICATIONS:

Quantity discounts are available on bulk purchases of this book for reselling, educational purposes, subscription incentives, gifts, sponsorships, or fundraising. Special books or book excerpts can also be created to fit specific needs such as private labeling with your logo on the cover and a message from a VIP printed inside.

Social Evolution

11037 Rio Vista Drive

Austin, TX 78726

To Mom

MOTIVATION: AN INTRODUCTION

At one time, Ts'ui Pen must have said, 'I am going into seclusion to write a book,' and at another, 'I am retiring to construct a maze.' Everyone assumed these were separate activities. No one realized that the book and the labyrinth were one and the same.
    - Jorge Luis Borges, from "The Garden of Forking Paths"[1]

Imagine for a moment you are about to set off on a bold adventure. You've been chosen from among thousands of candidates. Indeed, you are highly skilled and have been training for this for years. The adventure?

Go to Mars and start a colony.

Your days and evenings have been filled with preparation. You have had to learn all the ins and outs of space travel. Low gravity. Oxygen systems. Navigation. You have also had to learn what it takes to survive on a hostile planet. Radiation. Bitter cold. Sandy windstorms. But you're excited by the prospect of surviving on the surface of another world, and you have highly specialized skills to this effect. So despite the risks, you want to do this. You want it bad.

About a month out from launch, you get a visit from one of the officers at mission control. She says there's just one more thing she needs to find out before she can let you take off with the team.

"What do you want out of life?" she asks.

"Um," you hesitate, "to go to Mars."

"Is there nothing more fundamental than that?" she asks.

"Right now? I don't think so," you say.

"Well, why do you want to go to Mars?" she asks.

You get nervous. It occurs to you that the wrong answer to this question could get you kicked off the mission. So you raise your index finger as if to say, 'let me think.' then you scratch your head and reflect for a moment. You consider fame, but that's not it. You think about money, and that's not it either because being rich is way more fun back on earth. There's only one answer, and you're just going to have to be honest.

"It'll make me happy," you blurt out finally.

"Happy?" she says.

"Yeah. I don't see this as some sacrifice for the human race. I love my training. I love doing my job. I love the idea of pushing humanity forward. The thought of working every day to build something of this importance. Well, *that* will make me happy."

"Alright, colonist," she says, smiling. "I'll see you in a month."

Now, you might have a couple of questions about that story. You might even have some questions about the whole exercise. And that's understandable. Let me see if I can anticipate a couple of them.

First, why did the mission officer need to know that you were interested in being happy? Well, for one thing, you have to be motivated by something powerful enough to undertake such a dangerous mission. It's going to require a lot of you. A sanctimonious feeling of self-sacrifice would not last very long. For another, unhappy people can make everybody else pretty miserable. Your colleagues don't need that.

Second, why this story in particular? The truth is, I could have asked you to imagine starting a circus, scoring a symphony, or making a quilt. The framing could be pretty much anything. After all, why do any of us do just about anything? There are exceptions, but the answer almost always traces back to the same motivation: *the desire to be happy.* Even the unpleasant things like going to work or paying your bills have something to do with it because people who don't pay their bills become unhappy pretty quickly.

And that is a fitting place to start. I want to be happy. You want to be happy. (If not, you might want to see a therapist.) But assuming we both share this fundamental desire, we have found a nice green patch of common ground.

MARSHMALLOWS

It's pretty safe to assume that most of us are motivated by the desire to be happy. Sure there are some weird exceptions. Some people have psychological disorders that make them engage in self-destructive behavior. Others seem to resist happiness outright. But by and large, to be a well-adjusted human being is to seek happiness.

But what is happiness? It's a question philosophers and ordinary people alike have grappled with for millennia. And we should spend a little time with the concept because it's not as simple as it seems.

It's tempting, for example, to think of happiness as a mere sensation, like a good feeling. But it's more than that. Sure, positive emotions are part of it, but they're not the sum of happiness. The ancient Greek philosophers like Aristotle talked about *eudaemonia*, which includes a sense of general well-being but sprinkles in meaningful activity. Happiness can sometimes involve being in a state of engagement with something challenging, which positive psychologists call "flow." And of course, happiness can flow from pursuing and achieving your goals.

We shouldn't forget that connection to other human beings is important to our flourishing. Just as our happiness is compounded when we have others to celebrate with, our victories aren't as enjoyable when we are alone. Similarly, when we have the opportunity to help others directly, of our own volition, we can experience more profound happiness in giving.

Remember, though, happiness is not a discrete goal. It's a state of being. It takes dedication to maintain a state of being. If happiness flowed only at the point of attaining a goal, it wouldn't last long. So we are set up as humans to find happiness on the journey, too. In other words, it's not just the pursuit of happiness. It's also about happiness in pursuit.

At some point, we must all learn that sustained, higher-quality fulfillment rarely comes in the form of immediate gratification. And that's a good thing. If everything we did in life got rewarded with empty pleasures, we'd have died out as a species long ago. The caveman who idled but never hunted or foraged might feel good briefly, for example, but he would quickly suffer and starve. Similarly, the young person who spends her first year's salary on an expensive new car instead of saving might find that she has little left for retirement.

You might be familiar with the famous marshmallow experiment conducted with children. Researchers offered kids a choice between one small-but-immediate reward (a marshmallow), or two small rewards if they could wait a few minutes. In follow-up studies of the grown children, the researchers found that children who were able to wait longer for the marshmallow tended to fare better concerning various life outcomes. You might say they had more grit. And grit might be heritable, at least partially.

The marshmallow experiments are controversial and subsequent studies cast doubt on the original. Still, parents used the marshmallow study for years as a pop-psychological instrument of self-flagellation, as many of them decided their children were doomed. It turns out it might be far easier to *learn* deferred gratification than the original researchers thought. And if it is, that's a good thing.

All of us have to learn to defer gratification. It's that simple. And strangely, there can be added gratification in deferment. Some of us will be naturally better at it than others, but it can be an avenue for giving ourselves greater well-being in the future. For example, people put money into retirement plans so they don't have to worry about income when they are seniors. And, of course, most any worthwhile endeavor requires giving up the satisfaction of *right now* to have greater happiness in the future. If you're starting a business, you might have to eat peanut butter until you find investors. If you're going to become a university research scientist, you have to study hard and take tests you don't like until you earn an advanced degree. Often, the stuff that makes us happiest *now* required a lot of investment in the past. Such investments sometimes come at the expense of picnics, parties, and other peak experiences. But that's life.

If you want to think of happiness as your primary motivation in life, that means you have to figure out which secondary and tertiary missions are worthy of your time, effort, and sacrifice. Do you want to raise a family? Do you want to build a business? Do you want to learn to make art? Then you have to imagine happiness as being spread out into the future, because to some degree, the kinds of well-being you experience now might have been possible due to the seeds you planted years ago. So gaining useful knowledge might be interesting, but it can also create happiness for future-you as you apply the knowledge down the road.

We can put matters another way: Doing the right thing today is about putting happiness into a future happiness bank. You can draw too much from your happiness bank by making poor choices today, even if those choices give you immediate gratification. You might think I'm talking about saving money. Although that can certainly be true, I'm also talking about treating your body right with diet and exercise, learning skills, and developing habits that will give you both lifelong enjoyment and financial returns. Time, effort, and sacrifice require you to think not just about attaining your goals but deriving some measure of happiness from pursuing them.

One of the biggest keys to living a flourishing life is to do meaningful things. It helps if other people find what you're doing meaningful, too, but you can't always rely on others' approval. What's important is that you find meaning and that it pushes you forward, sometimes through unpleasant or painful obstacles. Indeed, the stoically minded believe that obstacles are not only inevitable, but offer us opportunities to become more excellent as we overcome them.

It is fashionable to practice *mindfulness* and *gratitude*. The wisdom traditions remind us that giving thanks for what we have can make us happier. I suspect that is probably true, even though there are other reasons to practice gratitude. Recall that to be mindful is to develop a presence of mind in any given moment. Then to be grateful is to appreciate what you have, even if it's modest, as opposed to longing for what you lack. It might seem contradictory, but on the one hand, we should think fairly frequently about our future happiness because it requires adapting our behavior today. On the other, we sometimes need a break from thinking about the future because it can involve stress. In being mindful and grateful in the moment, we take a few minutes to get our minds out of that *future orientation* to appreciate what we have.

The paradox here is that learning to be grateful and taking the time to appreciate what you have is a way of thanking your past self for caring for your present self. To be future-oriented requires effort and willpower, so gratitude practice is not meant to replace goal-directed action or planning. It is instead a way both to rest and to learn to enjoy a little of life *right now*, which is the only life we ever really have, in a sequence of right-nows. In the balance between the happiness of pursuit and the joy of now, we can *become* those beings who had at one point been those aspirational selves living in our imaginations.

In the thought experiment above, thinking *I want to be one of the first Martian colonists* offers a way to define yourself in relation to your aspirations and objectives. But after you've arrived on Mars and set up the colony, there must be something more. There is the day-to-day work of being a Martian colonist, solving problems, building things, and helping others. That also has to satisfy you, at least in some measure. You should also derive a sense of meaning from doing the work, which is part of happiness too—perhaps the most important part. If you only derived satisfaction from the *idea* of going to Mars, you would not be a good candidate. Because when you are eight months away from Earth, with space ferries running infrequently, you'd better find ways to appreciate the little things. This is one of life's secrets.

MEANING AND MASLOW

Now let's talk about this whole business of meaning. If you think about the vast expanse of space or the absence of our happy (or unhappy) selves in death, it is tempting to think life is meaningless and that our pursuit of happiness is fruitless.

But the secret is each of us gets to be the author of our own lives. Even if we aren't religious, or think that someday there will only be nothingness, we are alive now. We get to have experiences that amoebas, rocks, and guinea fowl will never have.

In those experiences, there is a trace—perhaps a story—that can outlive us and persist in the minds of others, at least for a time, before the heat death of the universe.

As I write this, I wonder whether this volume can survive me in the hearts and minds of others. I want to leave traces. There is meaning to be found in leaving traces, merely because an aspect of yourself survives death. Before we can talk more meaningfully about meaning-making, we have to talk about survival.

In 1943, psychologist Abraham Maslow proposed his famous hierarchy of human needs in a paper called "A Theory of Human Motivation." Variously, Maslow and his colleagues have proposed five to seven levels, which refer to staged motivations. Let's use the seven-level model:

1. **Physiological.** The drive for food, warmth, and sex.
2. **Safety.** The drive to feel secure, out of danger, and to have shelter.
3. **Social.** The drive to be liked, to belong, to have ties of affection.
4. **Self-esteem.** The drive to feel respected or recognized; to feel in control.
5. **Cognitive.** The motivation to learn, explore, have knowledge and understanding.
6. **Aesthetic.** The motivation to appreciate beauty, symmetry, and natural wonders.
7. **Self-actualization.** The motivation to flourish, to become what you are capable of by using your abilities to the fullest, to find fulfillment and meaning.

Maslow's theory describes what a person is motivated to do given any perceived lack, at least among the first few levels. For example, if one's stomach is empty, she experiences hunger and is thus driven to find food to satisfy that drive. Once the need is satisfied, the drive disappears for a time.

When the first four drives are satisfied, Maslow believed that one could work to satisfy upper-level motivations— namely cognition, beauty, and self-actualization. Of course, that doesn't mean people always do. Some people get lost in excess and ostentation. But the last three motivations are the ones that enable personal growth. When you fulfill them, you might be even more motivated. In other words, when you feel full, safe, and comfortable, you might turn to intellectual and spiritual pursuits. Upon learning something new, you might, in turn, become inspired to learn more about the subject or some adjacent subject. So even though the first four levels are relatively bounded, the next group is less so. Such allows us to grow in intelligence, wisdom, and positive self-concept. Levels in Maslow's hierarchy are not mutually exclusive. Most people bounce around in them, living a portion of their time at various levels each day. Just as you might need to take a break from reading this book to visit a friend or find warmth, I might have to eat a meal before I can resume writing these words. Everyone must spend at least a portion of their time in pursuit of satisfying their physical needs.

But a critical difference between humans and all other living organisms, arguably, is that animals spend the vast majority of their time pursuing the first two levels and little beyond. Humans, however, have figured out how to meet their basic needs more readily, so they can spend more time on activities that make for satisfaction at these higher levels. Simply put, humans can appreciate the beauty of a Shakespeare sonnet. It doesn't mean they always do, of course. Some people are unhappy even though they've met their basic needs. Still, humans are the only known species that can derive happiness from beauty, contemplation, and personal growth.

PRAXEOLOGY

The twentieth-century economist Ludwig von Mises developed a theory of human action that dovetails nicely with Maslow's work. Mises's theory, praxeology, rests on the idea that individual human beings act, which means they engage in conscious activities towards goals. Philosophers call this teleological behavior, and telos is another word for goal. Teleological behavior differs from reflex actions and, for Mises, a lot of social science can be predicated on this fundamental insight.

Because human beings act and their actions take place in

the service of various ends, we can surmise that most human behavior is varied but purposive. Different people pursue different paths to different ends. By implication, individuals have different values, which structure their various pursuits. Some values sit on the lower rungs of Maslow's hierarchy, while others sit near the top. But there is a law-like quality to these value-structured pursuits. This corresponds to the idea that people are motivated to achieve satisfaction through action. Mises's praxeology makes no judgment about the wisdom of anyone's goals, whether he should or should not eat the seed corn, for example. Interestingly, one might argue that Buddhists are praxeologists, too. The difference is that Buddhists practice *non-attachment,* which is a kind of satisfaction made possible by limiting unhealthy fixation on objectives. But practice is still action.

Praxeologists only hold that people have goals and think they can arrive at them by taking action. Actions can be right or wrong insofar as they help one achieve contentment or happiness. Furthermore, these actions take place in some set of circumstances over time. If one's desires could all be satisfied by snapping one's fingers, finger-snapping might be the sum of human action. But human action is purposive and varied. Such an insight does not preclude coordination or collaboration among those who share goals. Indeed, coordination and collaboration can be essential to flourishing. Mises's method reminds us that only individuals act, even if they decide to work in synchrony or specialization towards some end. Whenever a person acts rationally, she thinks her action will make some difference, that is, that she'll prefer some state of affairs to whatever condition results from doing nothing at all.

Because no human being is omniscient, especially when it comes to predicting the future, we all live in a world of uncertainty. In such a world we sometimes have to amend our behavior or change our plans. Happiness is never guaranteed. There is only the pursuit.

GRUB FIRST, THEN ETHICS

For most of human history, and certainly most of prehistory, people spent more time dealing with drives on the first three levels of Maslow's hierarchy. It wasn't until the Agricultural Revolution that the ancients could pursue intellectual and spiritual matters to such an unprecedented degree. In other words, Confucianism, Taoism, Zoroastrianism, and the Classical Philosophers all appeared in roughly the same era. And all were made possible thanks to the advent of settled agriculture, which made food more abundant, allowing people more time to reflect.

The surge in settled agriculture created opportunities for people to cluster. In cities, one might find scholars and priests who pondered the benefits of living together in harmony. What are the protocols and practices for living in peace? The ancients bequeathed us fragments of their wisdom, which we overlook at our peril. Even the scholars and priests had to fill their bellies before holding forth in the squares or scribing in the temples.

"Grub first, then ethics," said Berthold Brecht, famously. Perhaps there is no more concise way to discuss the regulatory function of our innate drives. But to solidify our understanding of the fundamental motivation human beings have to seek happiness, ask yourself: *Why are we driven to eat food or protect ourselves from harm? Why are we driven to seek out others with whom to associate?* At the most basic level, the answer is *to stay alive*. Being alive is the opposite of being dead. Yet, it bears repeating: To be dead means to be devoid of any physical or mental activity that would satisfy you. In this way, maximizing both your mental and physical energy towards the satisfaction of your drives makes you alive and, in some sense, more human by degree.

Of course, not everyone wants to spend time pondering the universe, writing books, or arguing in the agora. But there is something uniquely human about our ability to indulge these upper-level drives. We push humanity forward with cognition, aesthetics, and self-actualization. Such progress has had positive compounding returns for our species and will for future generations. But whether we are trying to survive out on the savannah or to look out over vast cities from skyscrapers, we are all united through time by one thing: We want to be happy.

BLISS MACHINE

Skeptics might argue that human happiness is not really any sort of prime motivator. Indeed, try asking folks if they would step into a bliss machine[2] that could make them 'happy' at every moment for the rest of their lives. Most would refuse.

But this refusal does not indicate people aren't motivated to find happiness. Instead, it means that there is a deeper meaning to be found when we face down struggles in the world and overcome challenges. Happiness without meaning is hollow. Happiness involves striving, and importantly, contact with reality.

COMMON GROUND

Polymath entrepreneur Chris Rufer says there is something fundamental about this desire to be happy. (This Introduction is an outgrowth of many conversations with Rufer, whom I consider a mentor.) But as our brief exploration shows, happiness can be hard to define. Maybe we can agree that even though it might take libraries to define happiness, and even though each of us faces different circumstances and constraints as we pursue it, we share common ground. That is to say that most of us not only seek to maintain a state of happiness in its many manifestations, but we want to live in conditions that are more likely to give rise to the big three. Rufer refers to them as *happiness, harmony,* and *prosperity*. In a certain sense, these conditions are all interdependent, as a kind of braid.

Happiness, broadly construed, tracks with our intuitions about just what humans are seeking as they pursue a good life. So happiness includes both the pleasurable (hedonic), which is narrow but expands to flourishing (eudaimonic), which is broad. The hedonic refers to pleasures such as eating a good meal, enjoying a fun experience, or engaging in sensual pleasures. The eudaimonic refers to the kind of experience one might find in fulfilling work, spiritual reflection, or practice towards excellence. As we suggested, people make tradeoffs between short-term pleasures and meaningful flourishing. The key is to find the right balance among pleasure, well-being, and meaning in life, wherever we are on our journeys.

Harmony, then, is a condition in which people live together peacefully. There is a general lack of discord, enmity, or violence in such a condition. People living in harmony might not particularly like one another or share personal values. They nevertheless tolerate one another and leave each other to pursue different conceptions of the good. Harmony is, in an important sense, the absence of social friction, which makes other forms of human interaction possible.

Prosperity generally means overall abundance, such as relatively greater access to the things that help people survive and thrive. But prosperity need not be defined as material wealth. It can also mean non-material plenty, such as leisure time, personal development, or the kind of social or spiritual rewards that flow in a condition of harmony. In this way, prosperity is not just a condition of financial wealth. It includes all the good things wealth affords us.

I suggested above that happiness, harmony, and prosperity are interdependent. For example, people in a state of harmony are more likely to collaborate effectively. So what about their opposites: unhappiness, disharmony, and poverty? When there is disharmony, the fires of conflict will start to burn and conflict creates suffering. The reverse can also be true: Unhappy people tend to cause more trouble, which leads to conflict. So, if harmony is a precondition for collaboration and exchange, it should be obvious that too much conflict increases poverty. And, of course, poverty creates headwinds to one's pursuit of happiness. These positive and negative interdependencies can create upward or downward spirals, respectively. Thus happiness, harmony, and prosperity should always be understood as working together.

Happiness without harmony is fleeting because there will soon be friction and strife. Happiness without prosperity is asceticism, a path which the Buddha himself abandoned. Prosperity without happiness is anxiety, loneliness, or fear. Prosperity without harmony is a world of unhealthy rivalries and gated homes sequestered from a community. Harmony without prosperity is a hungry group sitting around a campfire.

WHAT THIS BOOK IS ABOUT

Happiness is our preoccupation in this Introduction because, at some level, it is the core motivation. The big three – happiness, harmony, and prosperity – are good and are woven together. At the very least, we can say most of us share a desire for such conditions. If we cannot agree that finding some measure of happiness while we're alive is fundamental to being human, then the rest of this book is of no use, and perhaps the rest of our lives are of no use either.

I wanted to introduce this book with thoughts about the great motivator, because happiness is humanity's unmoved mover. We can slice it up in different ways: Is there pleasure to be found in an orgasm? Inspiration to be discovered in a book? Meaning to be made in our good works? Life is composed of answers to such questions.

But what does happiness have to do with articulating a doctrine? Everything. Our pursuits are various. So the systems in which we pursue happiness can't all be the same. Sometimes we walk together. Other times the path must fork. To the extent we can see life is a garden of forking paths, we have to create opportunities for people to blaze different trails.

I hope not to give too much away in saying that our mission is to create a condition of radical pluralism, a garden of forking paths. If you are familiar with the Argentine author Borges, I hope you will permit me to take some liberties with that phrase. That is, in our lives we sometimes play out seemingly incompatible storylines. These stories suggest bifurcation—splitting—whether of time, space, or association. And yet the whole human story will still be there. In our ideal future, the strutting and fretting characters come to a point where more than one outcome is possible. So it ought to be. Therefore, why shouldn't *many* outcomes be possible? This way of thinking causes our stories to branch out into multiple narrative universes, setting up opportunities for new bifurcations.

Decentralism then is not just about the functional idea of decentralization, breaking up political power, although that idea is central to our thesis. The idea, née the ideal, involves creating space for human beings to find niches that best suit their conceptions of the good life. But sometimes, one needs to create a new niche. In a world of great powers sitting on virtually all of the landmass covering the earth, new niches can be hard to come by. If our objective is to make room for the garden of forking paths, we must set about changing minds.

Dear Reader, if you would permit me, I'd like to start with yours.

1
MISSION: ONE REVOLUTION

Just as the technology of printing altered and reduced the power of medieval guilds and the social power structure, so too will cryptologic methods fundamentally alter the nature of corporations and of government interference in economic transactions.
  - Timothy C. May, from the "Crypto Anarchist Manifesto"[1]

IF THE PRIME motivation for every person is to pursue her version of happiness, the point of governance must surely relate to that pursuit. The American Founders were keenly aware of this, yet their experiment seems to have run its course. Around the world, the republics that borrowed from the Philadelphia rationale seem to be slouching the way of Rome. Still, the Founders were onto something. And we can look out on a new horizon perched upon their shoulders.

We need not occupy ourselves with history to say that

Alexander Hamilton, the great American Centralist, won the debate in 1789. Unfortunately, he lost the plot. The American Story is still playing out, but unless an intrepid few write a bold new chapter, the ending is not likely to be so happy. Centralism has corrupted America, and there is not likely to be another constitutional moment. There is no reboot button for a sclerotic republic. There is only the accretion of power, which is accelerating and has grown venal and topheavy.

We need a new mission. A revolution. It must be built upon a comprehensive doctrine that transcends and includes the Anti-federalist view of decentralizing power. The mission can't be some free-standing political ideal involving rationalistic fantasy or bloodless liberalism. Instead, it must take on the character of justice and religion, originating from within the human heart, where morality and meaning live. Without obliging its adherents to worship in the Church of Politics, embrace superstition, or dream up some Great Charter, this new society must be more the product of human action than of human design.

Our doctrine, Decentralism, is not just about digital currencies and smart contracts. It is a life philosophy. Technology is just a means of instantiating our life plans. In other words, despite an army of meddlers and middlemen standing in the way, Decentralists won't stop until we have reached our objective. We call that objective the Consensual Society.

It should sound familiar.

> Governments are instituted among Men, deriving their just powers from the consent of the governed, --That whenever any Form of Government becomes destructive of these ends, it is the Right of the People

to alter or to abolish it, and to institute new Government, laying its foundation on such principles and organizing its powers in such form, as to them shall seem most likely to effect their Safety and Happiness.

Our mission is to finish the job promised in the Declaration of Independence, realizing all the while that the Constitution, admirable as it is, has failed to deliver on that promise. We will have to create the Consensual Society niche by niche in many different places worldwide. In that cosmopolitan effort, we will construct our niches in both the digital cloud and on terra firma.

We can't have a dialog with Thomas Jefferson about how far he might extend the rationale of consent. The obvious difference is *ex-ante* versus *ex-post* consent, the latter of which Jefferson clearly intended. Would Jefferson agree with the idea that we should be allowed to opt into any governance system in advance? Or is he committed to the idea that some authorities should be allowed to impose their will on the people and those people have a right to amend or abolish the imposition later? I cannot say. Were he alive I would try to persuade him: Ex-ante agreement is a far better arrangement.

I suspect legal theorist Lysander Spooner would have agreed. He writes:

If any man's money can be taken by a so-called government, without his own personal consent, all his other rights are taken with it; for with his money the government can, and will, hire soldiers to stand over him, compel him to submit to its arbitrary will, and kill him if he resists.[2]

Though Decentralists wish to be free from state interference, we prefer technical means to political means in pursuing that mission. Politics, after all, is a rigged game. Thus Decentralism, in its antipolitics, is both a way of *seeing* and a way of *being*.

The Decentralist way of seeing is a general skepticism of all claims to political authority. Indeed, Decentralists in the liberal tradition are not only skeptical of authority, they think any right conception of justice ought to originate in consent. In other words, you should be able to choose your own governance association. No one else should be allowed to force any system on you. This philosophy contrasts starkly with either Lockean or Rousseavian conceptions that evoke a hypothetical social contract or general will.

Decentralists seek consent-based governance and reject compulsion. So, despite widespread sentimental attachments to the democratic republic, Decentralists think nation-states are unjustifiable. All systems rooted in compulsion or subordination are indefensible unless their citizens give prior consent.

Yet states exist. And that's because they can. So most Decentralists are under no illusions when it comes to the prospect of making a case to the powerful. We realize that political authorities are not likely to tolerate any form of peaceful association that challenges their power. And those who benefit from state transfers are not likely to withdraw their support from entities promising those transfers. So, state proxies and their supplicants have every incentive to fight for incumbency.

Therefore, the Decentralist thinks political authority exists, as any other phenomenon of nature exists, like hurricanes or malaria. To acknowledge this reality gives rise to the Decentralist *way of being*. That is, those who do not accept political authority simply have to find a way to navigate life with it as a social fact. And then *push back*. To *be* a Decentralist is to be comfortable with civil disobedience—all while creating consent-based systems in parallel. Such systems will be designed to challenge, circumvent, or obsolete political authorities.

You won't hear a Decentralist advocate violence, though we reserve the right of self-defense. Due to its nonviolent nature, Decentralists call their approach to social change "underthrow,"[3] the peaceful alternative to overthrow. Happily, our underthrow resembles another word that stands for the power of retreating ocean waters to sweep even the mightiest off their feet.

Decentralism is a sibling of crypto-anarchism, though the latter comes with a bundle of connotations that might frighten or confuse the unbaptized. The prefix "crypto" makes computer scientist Timothy C. May's moniker seem somewhat esoteric. Admittedly, there is secrecy in the conception. Otherwise, how will one evade the state's attention and control? The other connotation of 'crypto' is technical. It comes from cryptography, a set of tools fashioned by computer scientists and mathematicians. But, of course, these technologies have always been fashioned according to human desires for privacy or free association. In this way, cryptography innovators design systems that allow two or more parties to engage in unmolested and unmonitored communication, collaboration, and exchange. Protecting these forms of association is crypto-anarchism's *raison d'etre*. Decentralists are siblings in this regard. It's the 'anarchism' bit that could prompt some readers to run away screaming in nightgowns and curlers. So instead of parsing fine distinctions between crypto-anarchists and Decentralists, I'll use this volume to let Decentralism speak for itself.

Before we turn to Decentralism's precursors, I want to address a proverbial elephant. Decentralism is somewhat ideological, but it is primarily strategic. You might say it's 20 percent ideology and 80 percent strategy. If human happiness, harmony, and prosperity are ideological motivators, so be it. But arguments about some ideal order are silly and impracticable. Yes, we need our north star, but we also need to be keenly aware that powerful authorities will seek to thwart our efforts at every turn. Decentralism is then, at best, something like an asymptote, an effort that gets closer and closer to ideal but never arrives. And, indeed, its instantiations will never be perfect. Perfectionist doctrines are doomed. Instead, Decentralists embrace the mission and work relentlessly to create spaces to experiment in creating consent-based niches. We seek to lower the costs of exiting any system that does not serve its members. We seek to lower the costs of entering any system that promises better to serve its members. As liberal thinker Paul Emile du Puydt wrote in 1860:

> My panacea, if you will allow this term, is simply free competition in the business of government. Everyone has the right to look after his own welfare as he sees it and to obtain security under his own conditions. On the other hand, this means progress through contest between governments forced to compete for followers.[4]

As we experiment, we know some systems will fail. In this

respect, Decentralism is a meta-doctrine, one that includes the widest diversity of possible systems: a utopia of utopias. But some people will try to create systems based on bad ideas. Those systems will have to run squarely into the iceberg of reality.

HISTORY

Decentralism's history is long and storied. One can imagine secret societies that formed under tyrants in the days before mass communication.[5] We might even think of the American Antifederalists as proto-Decentralists.[6] And even though the Antifederalists lost the constitutional debate, their warnings turned out to be eerily prescient.

For the sake of brevity, let's situate the genesis of modern Decentralism at the dawn of the information age. In his famous manifesto, (Timothy C.) May anticipated everything from black markets to bitcoin. But it is in the latter that the true potential for Decentralism began to gestate in the minds of millions, not just a small group of cypherpunks.

In 2009, a person or group pseudonymously called Satoshi Nakamoto published the bitcoin white paper.[7] To Decentralists, the ramifications of this peer-to-peer digital cash system rival the printing press in significance. The bitcoin network is more than just an electronic cash system, though. It contains the germs of ideas currently being propagated more widely in code.

Today, there exists a dazzling evolutionary fitness landscape of tokens, smart contracts, distributed ledgers, and governance systems. Most importantly, bitcoin unleashed the idea that people could work together to construct new social operating systems without violence. Unlike nation-states, people can join or exit those networks at will, provided they honor any agreements they make.

Humanity began to envision the breakthrough in those early days: the convergence of tools and rules (technology and institutions). In *The Social Singularity*, I revived a phrase attributed to philosopher Marshall McLuhan:

> *We shape our tools, and then our tools shape us.*

Something like a corollary recommends itself:

> *We shape our rules, and then our rules shape us.*

As shapers of rules and tools, we know we will shape people, too. Prior to all this shaping, we want protocol designers to have been shaped to some degree by a strong moral sense. For the programmable incentives of the cryptocurrency revolution to be anything more than a contest among sophisticated Skinner boxes, both designers and users have to be better than rats.

As of this writing, thousands of cryptocurrency tokens represent various nascent technological ecosystems and their properties. Many of these systems demonstrate the power of disintermediation, which is a fancy way of talking about removing middlemen. Token ecosystems are a wonderland for the Decentralist. They represent the potential for self-organization according to as many experiments in living as there are different ideas of the good. Despite hackers and scammers, the "crypto" space holds the promise and possibility of transition into more consent-based systems of governance, which we call "rules without rulers." These technologies threaten to make powerful corporate and government hierarchies obsolete. Those who stand to be toppled are getting predictably hostile.

PERSPECTIVES

There is a decidedly libertarian flavor to Decentralist thinking. But many Decentralists reject libertarianism, and many libertarians reject Decentralism.

In drawing a crude map, you might think of libertarianism as a doctrine that includes a certain set of ideas about what kind of state authority is justified. For example, most libertarians accept some variation on the idea that one ought never to initiate harm against another person, which most Decentralists share. But libertarians imagine, like Locke or Hobbes, that a certain kind of centralized state power is necessary for the administration of justice—a benevolent monopoly on violence. So, like the American Founders, libertarians think the state is justified, but that officials must be limited in what they are permitted to do. Their police powers must be restricted to protecting lives and property, and nothing more.

The problem, of course, is how to oblige the state's agents to constrain themselves despite powerful incentives to the contrary. Checks and balances are necessary, but Decentralists put Madison's skepticism of political angels on steroids. As Edmund Burke said,

---

> In vain you tell me that [government] is good, but that I fall out only with the Abuse. The Thing! The

> Thing itself is the abuse! Observe, my Lord, I pray you, that grand Error upon which all artificial legislative Power is founded. It was observed, that Men had ungovernable Passions, which made it necessary to guard against the Violence they might offer to each other. They appointed Governors over them for this Reason; but a worse and more perplexing Difficulty arises, how to be defended against the Governors?[8]

Decentralists think the best check on power is more radical systems of permissionless decentralization. These forces give rise to opportunities to exit a system if it doesn't serve one's needs. In this way, Decentralists are pragmatic. While most see no contradiction in using both political- and non-political means to check unjustified authority, they prefer non-political means. Widespread civil disobedience is a more effective check.

The more people move into consent-based systems, the more likely they will generate a global market in governance services. The overall effect will be a less violent set of institutions, nation-states notwithstanding. After all, if one has to force people to obey some set of rules, that's far more costly and far less valuable than a body of law people choose and use, such as *Lex Mercatoria* or merchant law. This form of customary law results in real human interactions and agreements, which get tested and adjudicated over and over in courts. That's one reason why Decentralists believe in real social contracts, not hypothetical ones.

Decentralists also take issue with minimal statists (minarchists), to the extent the latter present a more rigid checklist for what constitutes a just society. Indeed, most Decentralists are more comfortable with the fact of pluralism, including *governance pluralism*. The idea is that given a chance, people would opt into systems that some libertarians would find illiberal. But the Decentralist understands it is reasonable to accept certain constraints on her behavior, say by contract, as long as she gets something important in return—including her idea of the social good. To live under her idea of the social good, she must accept others who do not.

It will not be easy to shake the mirage of the benevolent state, the incentives of state actors, and the old habits of politics, even if it *were* possible to create "minimal" states. Most voters treat their fourth-grade social studies books as some kind of scripture, which maintains a kind of civic mythology. And they pay their taxes, which allows them to outsource any remaining sense of civic responsibility to "representatives." They can then get on with the more mundane cycles of work, play, and online culture wars.

There are plenty of overlaps between minarchists and Decentralists, though important differences too. However one draws the map, the territory is stranger. Some Decentralists have an aversion to traditional corporate forms. The more leftish among them resist systems built on institutions of private property. Indeed, some Decentralists think that states aid and abet corporations and would like to see both types of hierarchies reformed or even abolished. Others don't go so far but are interested in how technological solutions like distributed ledgers can create alternative financial systems, such as time banking, mutual credit, and commoning.[9] Libertarian-leaning Decentralists are more interested in those systems that enable free exchange, voluntary association, and mutual aid[10] —not to mention tax avoidance. They leave room for private and common property to evolve as institutions.

Decentralists need not factionalize in the matrix of power, because the point of Decentralism is pluralism. Instead of the never-ending search for 'checks and balances,' Decentralists united under the idea of consent, which has the power to govern just about everything in a regime of governance pluralism. Not only are there opportunities for alliances, most Decentralists share certain basic commitments, including those from other magisteria, as we will see.

JUSTICE AS LAW

State actors are getting wise to systems that threaten their control. Powerful elites are developing an array of regulatory sticks and carrots to keep the herd timid. Regulators can drive many Decentralist solutions underground, including the most prosocial ones. Fear of the state's reprisals makes Decentralism too bitter a pill to swallow for the laity. After all, Decentralists operate either in legal gray areas or black markets, so waving a black flag is risky even if one is wearing a white hat. And, of course, authorities will paint Decentralists with the same brush as criminals who deal in vice.

"The State will of course try to slow or halt the spread of this technology," warns Timothy C. May in his original manifesto. State proxies will cite "national security concerns, use of the technology by drug dealers and tax evaders, and fears of societal disintegration."

May's predictions have been eerily accurate with the rise of cryptocurrencies.

One wouldn't want to suggest terrorist groups and drug traffickers don't use cryptographic tools; rather, one should point out that the most effective propaganda techniques almost always include grains of truth, which authorities exploit to justify crackdowns.

Most critiques of Decentralism turn on a confusion between *law as justice* and *justice as law*. In other words, a lot of critics think that deliberation among elected officials via the legislative process *creates justice* (law as justice). Whatever comes out of that legitimating process *is justice*. But Decentralists think this gets matters precisely backward.

Not only should different rulesets be tried and tested in frictions of human experience, something like law should only emerge from human interactions and agreements in which people discover justice. (Justice as law.) Consent-based law generates higher-quality law because finding justice is more of a discovery process than a deliberative one. Think: common law over statute law. In this way, the law becomes a happy byproduct of human choices, particularly as people seek to reduce friction with one another. Unfortunately, when legislators hand down statutes and force compliance, the discovery process gets short-circuited. The only feedback loop is the occasional election, which offers no guarantee of change, much less timely change.

CRITICISMS

Decentralist solutions are often illegitimate. This criticism is question-begging. As discussed, the nature of justice and law is at issue here. Whether an authority is legitimate is not the same as whether the authority is justifiable, either via philosophical inquiry or a decentralized discovery process. That is why the Decentralist's starting point for justice is consent.

Decentralist solutions are founded on a faulty conception of justice. This is an unsettled issue. Decentralists believe justice is a product of voluntary association. Whether they have the imprimatur of political authorities, systems of consent are both justifiable and just, as long as they cause no injury to anyone, within or without. Note that this is not the same as claiming that *if* an actor within some system brings harm, the system is wrong—a position some critics hold. Otherwise, to persuade a Decentralist that non-violent association is unjust is a great challenge. It is difficult to explain how injustice flows from two or more parties reaching agreements or making exchanges that harm no one. It's even more difficult for Decentralists to see how conceptions of justice that depend on coercion are more justified.

Decentralist systems make it possible for people to deal in vice. This statement is undoubtedly true, but does it work as a critique? While Decentralist solutions make it possible for certain people to facilitate wrongdoing, so do competing systems, especially state-sanctioned ones. This is not intended as a *tu quoque* argument. Instead, it is an invitation for critics to apply the same standards to their preferred systems. After all, when considering any system, we always have to ask: *As compared to what?* The *what* cannot just be some unrealized ideal. Decentralist systems are technological tools and institutional rules. Like more familiar tools, cryptography can be used in the service of good or evil. Hammers can be used to build a treehouse or murder one's spouse, but that latter fact does not make the existence of hammers unjustifiable.

Decentralist solutions make it possible for people to evade their responsibilities to the "common good." While it is also true that state authorities and statutes also make it possible for people to evade certain kinds of responsibilities, let's focus on the problem of what constitutes the common good. There are two ways to determine whether some "good" is common to members of a group: The first way is simply to claim that something is good and then attempt to justify authoritarian means of achieving that good. The second is to offer some purported good and then determine the extent to which people adopt it. Decentralists think demonstrated preference is superior to theoretical lip service, because people's actual choices supply proof. Solutions such as dominant assurance contracts show how consent-based provision of public goods can replace tax and transfer schemes, for example.

Decentralist solutions can be untransparent, making it challenging to hold bad actors accountable—especially when they initiate harm. Here again, we have to ask: *As compared to what?* We need to get into specific examples instead of just-so stories. One of the benefits of distributed ledgers and smart contracts is that they introduce systems that require less trust—whether in third parties or counterparties. For example, blockchains do a good job with escrow arrangements, proof of provenance, as well as providing pseudonymous identity and reputation systems. In this way, if two people are parties to a transaction, neither party needs to reveal her identity. Still, both parties will have strong incentives to have and keep a good reputation, which can be associated with a transacting pseudonym. These novel systems can balance privacy concerns against the benefits of cooperation. The ecosystems of cryptographic tech currently in bloom should never be dismissed due to failures of imagination. These ecosystems are growing, adapting, and poised to run rings around legacy systems that require police violence and standing armies to hold together.

REGIME ANCIEN

Even though most forms of Decentralism involve an ideological prior, such as consent, Decentralists tend to be highly pragmatic in the face of overwhelming power.

At Decentralism's core lies the realization that there is no One True Way. Despite powerful, entrenched legacy systems, Decentralists think the rapid evolution of technology, culture, and governance will shape the future. But expanding the range of non-violent human choices isn't likely to come about via legacy systems. The dynamics of interest-group politics and ideological warfare should disabuse people of such romantic notions. That is why Decentralists believe that, in the future, there will be more *governance pluralism*. In other words, people will be able to experiment with different systems no matter where they live. I call this cloud governance.

With greater decentralization, humanity will move into a condition that looks more like a free market in governance services. And that, by the way, is very different from claiming that any given system will be a free market. Why? Decentralization means people will join a system as one would an intentional community or civil association. Systems will compete for members.

Competition among providers of governance services offers three distinct benefits:

1. It humbly assumes there is no One True Way. People have different subjective preferences about governance systems. Pluralism is both a fact and an ideal.
2. It includes the idea that "the consent of the governed" ought actually to mean something beyond the abstractions of political philosophers.
3. It enables people to join economic or social niches according to their particular conceptions of the good (while acknowledging that one's conception may fail to attract and retain members).

The radical shift will be that governance services—including economic systems—are systems entrepreneurs will offer instead of being systems that authorities impose.

In this way, you can think of Decentralism as a meta-doctrine, but not a doctrine *per se*. Because it is a commitment to experimentation and choice, the only doctrinal aspect is the consent requirement. People will try out different systems. Not all systems will succeed. That's as it should be because the threat of member defection means evolutionary forces—not to mention hard reality—test each system. The best and most sustainable systems will stick around.

Eventually, there may be conflicts among systems. People will demand adjudication services, which will emerge and co-evolve within and between different governance systems. We will have to be more reflective in determining which features comport with our idea of the good in this condition. But that's a good thing. By lowering exit costs, we will join the system we prefer—whether communist, capitalist, or something altogether different.

The big tradeoff is that no one will be able to impose the One True Way on everyone else.

2
MEANS: TWO HANDS

The key to making people's lives better is knowing when coercion will work and when it would be best to leave people alone to cooperate. Given the complicated nature of human life, it should come as no surprise that this is not a simple, binary choice.

- James Harrigan and Antony Davies, from *Cooperation and Coercion*[1]

IN CHINESE MARTIAL ARTS, *Bao Quan Li* means 'fist wrapping rite.'[2] Maybe you have seen two fighters salute one another in their practice. Each stands up straight, clenches his right fist, and the four left fingers make a plane. Then, each places the two hands in front of his chest before wrapping the fist tight.

Bao Quan Li is a gesture that symbolizes discipline and restraint. Specifically, each of the four fingers of the left hand represents virtue, wisdom, health, and art. The bent thumb represents humility. The right hand, balled tight into a fist, represents power and action potential. When one brings these together, they represent rigorous practice and the responsible use of force.

Ponder this centuries-old symbolism as you consider the following, specifically about how societies change or constitute themselves: There are only two ways to get another to do what you want him to do—*compulsion* and *persuasion*. There is no other way. You can get someone to do something through lying or trickery, but these are just vicious forms of persuasion. You can calmly and gently inform someone that you have a gun, so they must open the till, but that's just polite compulsion.

In other words, one is left free to make her own decisions, or she is not. The world runs on compulsion and persuasion, and the preponderance of either in a society shapes it utterly.

1. COMPULSION

When you compel someone to do something, you threaten him with violence. *Do it or else.* The *else* is never pleasant. Indeed, it causes suffering. Yet, two entire magisteria are organized around these threats, although we don't always think of them as so constituted. The first magisterium is crime, which is intuitive because it is the domain of individuals making others worse off through some injury. Most of us wish to avoid those who would injure us, as criminals threaten our bodies, property, or reputations. The second magisterium, though, is politics, which is less intuitive. What do elections and legislatures have to do with compulsion?

Well, everything.

Whenever we refer to politics, we usually think of strategic games in which certain people jockey to access power and control. Ultimately, though, power and control are asserted through violent means. Voting supplies the illusion that each of us has a piece of that power, but your vote is a teardrop in the ocean, which is why the tide never seems to turn. By being born on a particular patch of soil, a special group of people gets to tell you what you can and cannot do. Others are paid enforcers. The rest obey, *or else*. If you disagree, the enforcers will come with guns and take you to prison. That means politics is more or less a complicated zero-sum game that cannot exist without the threat of violence.

It is a mistake to view crime and politics as non-overlapping magisteria, but we shouldn't dwell on matters too long. We might come to realize that politics is little more than a vast criminal enterprise that has simply legitimized itself. How are state authorities appreciably different from a mafia? Mafiosos divide the spoils among the family. Favor-seekers divide the spoils among those bidding in the lobby.

Most folks don't think of things this way. Inured as they are to state power figuring so comprehensively into their lives, they either conclude it has to be this way or that there is nothing they can do. People put up with authority as a Jew puts up with Christmas carols in November.

What can you do?

Subconsciously, people need to think of government as being staffed with angels who have their best interests at heart. Even if too few come to see politics as a protection racket wrapped in pomp and circumstance, perhaps we can at least agree there is plenty of overlap between crime and politics.

2. PERSUASION

When you persuade someone, you appeal either to his sense of right, or to his interests, or both. Two distinct magisteria arise from this approach. When you appeal to someone's sense of what's right or good, we call that *morality*. When you appeal to what you think she might like, we call that *marketing*. Morality and markets run on persuasion. Their watchword is *ought*.

You ought to abstain from stealing. (Morality)
You ought to buy that book. (Markets)

With morality, you're trying to guide your counterpart into a sense of what is right and wrong, so he acts accordingly. In markets, you endeavor to show a customer that something is desirable so he'll come to desire it and then act based on that desire. At no point are you making any threats.

Ought respects choice. *Or else* does not.

If one were playing semantic games, he might argue that threatening violence is just an unpleasant form of persuasion. But the point at which a decision-maker realizes his choice is between injury or acquiescence, he knows very well he's being compelled. What makes compulsion fundamentally different from persuasion is that compulsion limits autonomy and causes suffering.

TODAY WE LIVE in a regime of systematic compulsion supervised through a digital panopticon. But should we? Remember the dead religion Manichaeism, with its stark understanding of light and dark, good and evil. One might conclude from the discussion to this point that we're Manacheaian, that is, that compulsion is universally bad, and persuasion is universally good, at least as a means of getting someone to do something. After all, we have already stated that our mission is to realize the Consensual Society.

To address these concerns adequately, we need to strike a position between the absolute and the arbitrary.

An extreme position is that compulsion is never justifiable.

Yet hardly anyone would assent to such a view. Someone has to make children brush their teeth and stay out of traffic. Someone has to compel contract signatories to honor their commitments. And we certainly have to defend ourselves from those who would harm us. So if there is any room for compulsion in the Consensual Society, we have to be careful to circumscribe it, as the wrapped fist.

An arbitrary position might be that compulsion is justifiable relative to the interests of the stronger (might makes right) or relative to some culture's norms (cultural relativism). A brutal dictator claims everything he utters is God's will, and his people must obey his commands. Faraway people engage in genital mutilation because of various totems and taboos in their society. A cabal of mullahs decides homosexual acts shall be punishable by death. And in your more enlightened society, some will argue authorities should compel people for the 'common good.'

Between the absolute and the arbitrary, we want to find a sweet spot that puts compulsion in its place. We can start by proscribing the *initiation* of violence (or threat of violence) against those who have injured no one. We can add that people can and should be allowed to opt into different systems of association that constrain their choices and place obligations on them. The rest is conflict resolution. While these systems might require some internal compulsion, there are reasonable limits.

Consider that a good many people are willing to live in homeowners associations (HOAs). Maybe they value the manicured lawns and the brick facades more than they value being able to paint their homes neon purple and decorate their yards with plastic flamingos. But the HOA is not for everyone. And neither is the democratic republic with its ballooning military and grotesque transfer state. Most of us have been inculcated with a steady diet of civic lore about this form of government.

Maybe it's the best we've got, but we can do better.

For thousands of years, most of the world has lived under some form of military dictatorship. When Thomas Hobbes came along and told us why he thought that was a good idea, we bought it. And most still do to some degree. Sure, Locke and Montesquieu came along with their checks, balances, and natural rights, but that only replaced kingly caprice with special-interest capture. Throw in a couple of election spectacles, *et voila*—you've got a more tolerable form of serfdom.

MONSTROUS MORAL HYBRIDS

In *Systems of Survival*, urbanist Jane Jacobs explores the compulsion and persuasion paradigms. Jacobs explains what she regards as two fundamental survival strategies, which she calls "Guardian Syndrome" and "Commercial Syndrome." Either people can take what they need from other people through the threat of violence, or they can produce and exchange what they have to get what they need. Each approach comes along with a cluster of associated values. The raiders of Guardian Syndrome tend to express values, such as loyalty and pecking order, but shun persuasion's sweet talk. The traders of Commercial Syndrome tend to value hard work and inventiveness but are hesitant to threaten violence.

A curious thing happens when the syndromes are combined. Jacobs calls these "monstrous moral hybrids." What foul offspring slinks from the coital bed of business and government?

- Pharmaceutical corporations and regulatory agencies that collude to prevent data transparency and product liability while authorities mandate the company's experimental products;
- Military contractors whose revenues are made almost entirely of taxpayer largesse, giving rise to the military-industrial complex;
- Financial institutions designated 'too big to fail' reap massive profits in good times but receive heavy subsidies in bad times and benefit first from the Federal Reserve's quantitative easing.

Monstrous moral hybrids comprise a large portion of the world's economy.

Despite such unholy alliances, we have slowly moved away from compulsion as a primary means of social organization and change. The glacial pace is partly due to the inertia of these hybrid legacy systems. We can also credit our quiet failures of imagination, which bias us to the status quo. However, in this chapter I try to demonstrate another possibility, which is struggling to exist and exert itself. The way of consent is the way of liberation. The way of persuasion is the way to flourishing.

Can we accelerate our journey towards persuasion-based governance, fist in palm?

3
MIND: THREE GOVERNORS

For sale: baby shoes, never worn.
  - attributed to Ernest Hemingway

BEGINNING, middle, and end. Such is the architecture of a story and indeed of life. Humans orient themselves in time using past, present, and future. And though the triune God of Christianity has divine aspects in the Heavenly Father, the Incarnate Son, and the Holy Spirit, the spiritual significance of *three* is evident in nearly every culture.

Indeed, there are three yogas in the Vedic tradition: Jnana, Bhakti, and Karma. These are the paths of *knowledge*, *devotion*, and *action*, respectively. Perhaps unwittingly, the Russian mystic George Gurdjieff built an entire triadic typology atop this fundamental three in the Enneagram, which gives rise to nine types. But at its foundation, it is still *head*, *heart*, and *gut*.

That sacred three exists within each of us, too. Call them the Three Governors. Typically, each person has a primary:

- People of the *head* are thinkers who focus primarily on gaining and sharing knowledge.
- People of the *heart* are relaters who deal mainly in relationships and emotions.
- People of the *gut* are movers who are motivated to act or lead.

If we are to achieve flourishing, we need them all. The way to wisdom involves disciplining oneself to access the secondary and tertiary Governors and to braid them. The way to success involves working with others who have a different primary Governor, as we'll see.

Before dismissing these insights as artifacts of old religions, we should take the time to appreciate their power. After all, Decentralism involves empowering people to make good decisions and collaborate more readily. When it comes to making decisions or working collaboratively, aligning the Three Governors is essential to the Decentralist project.

1. HEAD

Cognition. If you suspect your primary Governor is the head, ask yourself what your process is when you decide. Do you tend to observe and analyze? Do you form a hypothesis in your mind and turn it over to decide on a course of action? If so, your primary Governor is probably the head. It might even strike you as odd that there would be any other Governor for making decisions. After all, reason and rationality developed in the neocortex for humans, a center situated squarely within the skull at the front of the brain.

But reason and rationality alone simply won't cut it. In the famous case of Elliot,[1] physicians removed a brain tumor that severed the connection between his reasoning brain (frontal lobe) and earlier-evolved modules. During recovery, people close to Elliot thought the patient was no longer himself. He became distracted and indecisive, sometimes analyzing the simplest tasks for hours. In short, he could no longer make decisions effectively, or better, *affectively*. While most of us are raised to think it's best for us to make decisions in moments of dispassion and calm reflection, we cannot separate how it *feels* to decide, which involves our other Governors.

Likewise, though brain scans revealed isolated damage to the ventromedial portion of Elliot's frontal lobe, he fared well on IQ, memory, and language tests. The problem lay with his emotions. In short, when viewing emotionally charged images, Elliot felt nothing. Neuroscientists now understand a critical intimacy between one's frontal lobe and, say, the limbic system. So many of our emotional responses depend on our limbic brain, which helped our forebears survive in dangerous circumstances. But we don't need neuroscientists to prove it. We know, *intuitively*, that there is a relationship between desires and decisions, for example.

2. HEART

Emotion. People whose primary Governor is heart will often be attuned to their emotions and that of others. They tend to be good at building and maintaining relationships because this attunement allows them to see how diverse people might connect or how they might clash. While heart types tend to be concerned with how people perceive them, sometimes overly so, their image consciousness can also be a boon to their careers or friendships. Some in this group become super connectors who help complementaries find one another.

There is, of course, a complex interplay between our brains and bodies when we experience emotions.

And, indeed, there is a strange relationship between our mental lives and our physical bodies. Even something as simple as a pain in one's arm will have a corresponding neural firing pattern in her head, which can be tracked using brain imaging. It appears our brains are evolved to represent features of the world or damage to our bodies, but our bodies are evolved to represent our emotions, as well.

Have you ever been heartbroken? If you've had to endure a romantic breakup, you might be familiar with what neuroscientist Antonio Damasio refers to as a somatic marker. That means the locus of emotional distress feels quite literally as if it is in your chest. Likewise, it's common for people to pull their hands close to their chests when they experience positive emotions, such as romance or baby cuteness.

Whatever the mysteries of consciousness, our feelings process vital information that we ignore at our peril. Sometimes, a decision just *feels* right, even if we can't articulate its justification. And there are times when we feel anxious, depressed, or uneasy for no apparent reason. Our feeling Governor is almost always trying to tell us to look more closely at our circumstances to see if something is wrong. In these cases, it's essential to *listen to one's heart* before repressing emotions or turning to pharmaceutical intervention.

The key is not to let the heart Governor exclude the other Governors from the decision-making process. Those who do will act out behaviors that resemble those of lower primates. Crimes of passion, for example, originate from failures to gain input from the gubernatorial committee. So even though our emotional center has much to contribute, we must be prepared to include our cognition and intuition, as well.

3. GUT

Intuition. Those whose primary Governor is the gut are about getting things done. They are leading the charge when they're at their best, but they can execute in the manner of ready-shoot-aim when at their worst. Some might describe the gut type as bold or brash, but she tends not to hesitate, and one might find her out front taking action. She knows how to trust her instincts.

The gut Governor is instinctual energy but expresses itself more as intuition than emotion. Remember that we cautioned against letting our emotions burn out of control, as can happen with animals. Such is true for instincts, too. At the same time, animals 'know' things we do not, though we wouldn't exactly call that faculty higher cognition. Such accounts for when dogs bark at a distant stranger we haven't yet noticed or when forest animals run away from a terrible storm before we have seen the leaves' undersides. When we speak of gut instinct, there are people in whom that force is more potent.

Those whose primary Governor is the gut can be intimidating. They'll employ what seems to be an inner power or sheer will to drive their behavior exactly where they want to be in life. This will come across to others as an excessive desire for control, and frequently it is. Gut types can respond to a perceived loss of control with frustration and anger, which can take over and cause chaos because they do not think before acting. Again, this is where the other members of the gubernatorial committee (mind and heart) can help.

ALIGNMENT

As above, there are two forms of alignment. The first is internal alignment, in which one practices tapping into the energies of the other Governors before taking action. The second is alignment among people who have different primary Governors. Both forms are critical to thriving in the Age of Complexity. Indeed, the Decentralist understands she will have to make adjustments as she adapts to waning centralization and waxing decentralization.

For example, decentralization amounts to more localization of decision-making authority. As more and more spheres of life require our input or action, positive feedback loops, both good and bad, will require our attention. Attention implies agency. In other words, as more decisions are *not* being made on our behalf, we must train up our sovereignty to face those decisions. That is why it bears repeating: Freedom and responsibility are two sides of the same coin.

If decentralization means more localization, there will be more experimentation and organization. Entrepreneurship, which requires people coming together in service of a mission, requires cooperation. It's tempting for so-called 'like minds' to come together for some venture, but this is usually a mistake, at least as it applies to the Governors. Organizations need people with different foundational energies and ways of perceiving the world. Why not birds of a feather? One might be tempted to organize as like-minded individuals, but that could be an error. Three head types can suffer from analysis paralysis. Three heart types can fail due to unprofitable generosity. And three gut types can be rash or competitive. You are almost always better off founding a complementary team that weaves head, heart, and gut energies into a more resilient braid.

The mode and manner of effective communication require

attention to the Three Governors, too. Consider the following three presentations as an account of a single event:

- On August 6, 1945, 129,000 people died after an atomic bomb was dropped on the city of Hiroshima.
- Yoshi returned to the village to find his wife, Himari, blistered and sick. Charring and debris were all that was left of his home. "You have always been my—" she muttered, but Himari was unable to finish the sentence before she expired in his arms.
- Yoshi's home is destroyed, so he's going to need somewhere to stay while he grieves. Maybe someone can take Yoshi to his brother's village nearby so he can get help with funeral arrangements.

It should be obvious that in one instance, we get the facts in the abstract; in another, we get a scene that should elicit some empathic response, and in the remaining presentation, we get clear calls to action. Effective communicators might combine these presentations into a kind of gestalt that allows us to represent the event humanely and holistically.

Some masters communicate with great concision to our head, heart, and gut. Hemingway's shortest story in the epigraph to this chapter might be considered a meme. Its memetic power comes in its appeal to the Three Governors.

One suspects that is precisely how one ought to communicate with moral suasion, too. In fact, moral philosophers who argue that their work is just Reason are kidding themselves. One can no more assert the rightness or wrongness of some action without the heart and gut as Elliot can make a decision about what music to put on. We are creatures of embodied cognition. And we were forged in evolutionary fires over millions of years. If we are better to govern ourselves, the goal is not to deny any of the three Governors, but rather to ensure each has a seat at the table.

4
MATRIX: FOUR FORCES

Of living things, my son, some are made friends with fire, and some with water, some with air, and some with earth, and some with two or three of these, and some with all.
   - Isis, from the *Hermes Trismegistus*

I must not fear. Fear is the mind-killer. Fear is the little-death that brings total obliteration.
   - Frank Herbert, from *Dune*[1]

MASCULINITY AND FEMININITY ARE ABSTRACTIONS, but they are not merely social constructs. They are properties programmed into the complicated facts of an evolved species whose biology we don't fully understand. Yet we know enough.

If children's play instincts are indeed a trial run of adulthood, evolution has distinct ideas about what kinds of things men and women will do, whether we like it or not. One need only observe a group of toddler girls and boys playing together in a room full of toys. The boys, on average, will be more likely to build it up and tear it down. The girls, on average, will be more likely to wait for their turns and select soft, cuddly toys. Boys are more likely to push others aside to get to a machine-like toy, and girls are more likely to take an interest in people and faces. Adults are not so different.

These proclivities can be enhanced or muted in the face of fear. Whether we are afraid of disease, scarcity, or death—our human energies roil within us, thanks to evolutionary pressures. Our job is not to deny these energies exist but to master them for the good of all. Now, even a cursory view of history reveals which sex is most likely to start a war or attempt to reign supreme by dominating others. Of course, history is also replete with tales of clever women manipulating powerful men. Still, if we were to throw a statistician's stone into a crowd, we are far more likely to hit a plunderer, fighter, or megalomaniac who is male.

Genetics, endocrinology, and neurology make men more likely to possess these *fuck-fight-force* dispositions, so we associate masculinity with the properties of this physiological substrate. Likewise, we associate femininity with women for reasons that wayward philosophers cannot simply deconstruct. Not only are women more likely to be empathic, but their primary disposition set is *flirt-fawn-facilitate*. Such energy has a physiological substrate.

Masculinity: fuck-fight-force

Femininity: flirt-fawn-facilitate

If one had to sum up masculinity in a word, it would be *forcefulness*. If one had to sum up femininity in a word, it would be *flow*. It's no accident that these correspond to the Two Hands, *compulsion* and *persuasion*. Without instantiation mediums, though, force and flow are but abstractions. So we have to consider masculine and feminine in the context of living beings who organize themselves in various ways according to their behaviors. Of course, both dispositions live in men and women alike, to varying degrees. As Carl Jung reminds us, like yinyang, we are vessels for the *animus* and the *anima*.

Admittedly, I invite readers to make some inferential leaps about these energies, which I refer to in largely metaphorical terms. Far from dismissing these patterns, which originate in our biological natures, we must confront them as we would any other truth. Our reference to energies, and later "forces," is designed as a helpful heuristic at this level of description. Otherwise, this chapter would become a tortuous research program. We must leave that to scientists. For now, a matrix of metaphors will have to do.

Now, let's turn to another duality of energies Sigmund Freud introduced that is intimately related. Modern psychologists, especially neuroscientists, are skeptical of Freud's ideas, despite his status as the father of psychoanalysis. Yet, virtually everyone acknowledges the existence of constructive and destructive psychological states, which is enough for our purposes.

To wit, Freud offers *Eros* and *Thanatos*,[2] which he explains are not strict, separate binaries but move together in the dance of our existence.

Eros drives us to live, to create, and to procreate. We exert ourselves through passion, or we give of ourselves through nurturing. Eros can take the form of ambition or yearning, but what we long for is a *genesis*. Creation. It is the wellspring of anticipation, as early Spring.

Thanatos, on the other hand, is the death drive. We seek to dissolve, to destroy, or to die. And though Thanatos can take an aggressive or a depressive form, we long for a *terminus*. Destruction. It is, as in late Fall, the expectation of absence.

Even though he was mistaken about a great many things, let's assume Freud was mainly correct about this duality. Draw a line in your mind that goes from Eros to Thanatos, which you can also call *creative* to *destructive*. An *x*-axis. Now, imagine another dimension, a *y*-axis of energies, which goes from masculine to feminine. The point is that human beings have the drive to create and the drive to destroy, *and* we are bundles of masculine and feminine energies. What happens when we combine them?

We arrive at the Four Forces.

Now we have a two-by-two matrix with four quadrants. Or, more simply, Eros and Thanatos each have dual aspects, which are masculine and feminine.

1. EROS MASCULINE

Eros Masculine is the urge to control. If things aren't going your way, you have to *make* them go your way. It's the way of force. It's the way of rock and iron, which can be used to defend the weak, jail the criminal, and build where there had been nothing. Eros Masculine involves competition and sometimes coercion. It can be forceful, but ultimately it wants to be foundational, stubborn, or stable.

Have we run out of space in the city? Let's build something tall, like a phallus, right into the sky. Think yours is tall? Mine will be taller. Make it so.

Earth represents the Eros Masculine. This symbol, an ancient element found in many cultures, calls to mind *Chi* in the Japanese philosophy *godai, and Chi* suggests solidity. So the

Eros Masculine manifests in forceful but generative behaviors, but it can also manifest as strength in controlling others, whether in the interests of order, stability, or outright suppression.
Exert control.

2. THANATOS MASCULINE

Thanatos Masculine is the urge to annihilate. If things aren't going your way, you must destroy what is in the way. This is the path of naked aggression. It's the way of fire. The fire warms our camp within the circle of stones, but we endanger the camp if we remove the stones. Thanatos Masculine scorches the earth.
Their way of life is at odds with ours. They are the enemy. Bring fire down upon their village.

Thanatos Masculine can be a white-hot rage that takes us to war or, at home, a passion that threatens even those we love.

Ka, the fire symbol in *godai*, represents combustion or a rapid energy release state change, such as an explosion. Similarly, we can symbolize Thanatos Masculine with fire, which is easy to associate with destruction and war. The fire need not be that of a literal war between peoples. It can also manifest in immediately, perhaps rashly, firing someone from his job or ending a relationship with words that make reconciliation impossible. Thanatos Masculine is about destruction.
Burn it down. End it now.

3. EROS FEMININE

Eros Feminine is the urge to flow. If things aren't going your way, it's okay if they go another way, or maybe they'll come around to your way in time. It's the way of persuasion and persistence, and it's the way of water.

Sui, the water symbol in *godai,* represents liquid. In markets, liquidity refers to the ease with which an asset or security can be converted into something else without affecting its price. Otherwise, liquid coheres but is flexible. It morphs and changes despite obstructions, like a stream around pebbles and boulders alike.

In nature, almost everything flows in a vascular fashion. River basins, circulatory systems, and the roots and branches of trees all express this phenomenon. Call it the Law of Flow, following physicist Adrian Bejan:

"For a finite-size flow system to persist in time (to live) it must evolve such that it provides greater and greater access to the currents that flow through it."[3]

The earth's surface is seventy percent water, just as our bodies are seventy percent water. As the moon tugs the tides, we are but complex extensions of life's flows. Eros Feminine facilitates, perhaps as a fluid that lubricates the necessary parts. It fawns, nurtures, and tames. Eros Feminine is about care and especially about persuasion. This concept is vital to understanding living systems and, indeed, decentralization.

Let it flow.

4. THANATOS FEMININE

Thanatos Feminine is the urge to rest. If things aren't going your way, just go to sleep or stay in bed. It's the way of withdrawal, and it's the way of the night. At night we sleep to recover from the day, but our final rest is in death. Melancholy wraps us in times of sorrow as we grapple with loss or grief. Thanatos Feminine reminds us that all good things must come to an end.

Fu, the wind, symbolizes vapor or air in *godai*. Likewise, we use the element air to symbolize Thanatos Feminine. Morbidly, one usually learns of death from the air first, as the dead decompose. We also associate air with absence, yet it is never wholly absent. Air aspires to absence, and the very word 'aspire' derives from the Old French *aspirer* "to inspire; breathe, breathe on."[4] Sometimes headwinds push against us as we struggle forward on a journey. Tailwinds can propel us to a voyage's end. A single audible out-breath can mark the end of a day. And a sigh can mark the end of a conversation.

Breath is associated with life, too, for without it, we would die. But when we *expire*—which is to breathe out—it reminds us of death's inevitability. So the breath of life implies the breath of death or expiration. In this way, maybe we can become more comfortable with the cyclical nature of existence.

Otherwise, Thanatos Feminine is sleepiness after a weary struggle or the weight of depression's torpor. It weakens us but calls us to lie down. Thanatos Feminine is about endings.

Good night, my love. Let things go.

IMBALANCE

Again, the tendency is for men to be motivated primarily by masculine energy and women to be motivated by feminine energy. But both energies are present in each of us by degree, expressed through our drives to create and destroy. It is when we fail to confront our fears with reason that we allow the Four Forces to get out of balance.

The wise seek to bring the Four Forces into balance, recognizing that all such energies have healthy and unhealthy expressions. The Decentralist seeks systems that allow participants to strike a healthy balance.

A healthy home, then, is one in which the couple strives to

become like the Hindu god Ardhanarishvara, the *unified* manifestation of Shiva and his consort Parvati. This being is both male and female. Likewise, a healthy society balances those self-same energies.

And yet another manifestation of Parvati is Kali, the goddess of time, death, and endings. Lord Shiva shows up from time to time as the destroyer. The cycles of beginnings and endings will turn in the fullness of time, just as surely as the sun will set on the centralized order.

These Four Forces affect human behaviors, which give rise to our human systems. In other words, these forces become instantiated in our cultural outlook, our institutions, or in the invisible patterns of life that comprise our social reality.

The Four Forces are paired with their associated symbols and imperatives.

- **Eros Masculine**—(earth)—*Exert control.*
- **Thanatos Masculine**—(fire)—*End it now.*
- **Eros Feminine**—(water)—*Let things flow.*
- **Thanatos Feminine**—(air)—*Let things go.*

Each quadrant in this matrix of human energies and drives has healthy and unhealthy expressions. It's not merely that imbalances among the Four Forces can predominate, but we can manifest unhealthy aspects of each Force. Imbalance means an excess of one or more forces, and an unhealthy manifestation can be applying a Force where it doesn't belong.

It can be tempting, for example, to upbraid a new colleague sternly as if that will offer the appropriate corrective. Rather than being corrected, she might come to feel defeated and demeaned, which is not likely to enhance her performance. Instead, maybe we can anticipate her beginner's mistakes and provide room for her to grow in her new role. In this case, we might choose to *let things flow* and *let things go* until the colleague learns.

Consider some examples of the Four Forces in healthy and unhealthy expressions:

Eros Masculine
Unhealthy: An overbearing boss who barks orders or micromanages.
Healthy: An inspiring coach who leads a team to victory.

Thanatos Masculine
Unhealthy: A dictator who assassinates his political rivals.
Healthy: A person who quickly ends a dangerous relationship.

Eros Feminine
Unhealthy: A person who indulges irresponsibly or to excess.
Healthy: A parent who lets his child try things and learn from mistakes.

Thanatos Feminine
Unhealthy: An entrepreneur who gives up on her venture prematurely.
Healthy: A aged grandparent who leaves a do not resuscitate order in hospice.

I write this volume at the cusp of the Age of Complexity. At this cusp, centralized systems must begin to give way to decentralized systems because centralized systems require controllers. In other words, the masculine must give way to the feminine.

Society has become too complex for controllers to exert control, yet control is the essence of Centralism. Severe unintended consequences and information breakdown will become commonplace as authorities double down on the will to power. If they persist in clinging too tightly to the notion that control is possible, Decentralists will underthrow them. Otherwise, we will all be cast into a Dark Age.

Thus, we must teach ourselves how to relate to one another peacefully without central control.

Currently, though, the world is out of balance. Specifically, Eros and Thanatos Masculine suppress the flow systems of Eros Feminine and Thanatos Feminine. That means the urges to control and to annihilate are too strong. Those seeking to *exert control* or *end it now* would be better to *let things flow* and *let things go*. The trouble is that Centralism is irredeemably masculine.

Complexity is feminine. It's no wonder all the undesigned ecologies of the planet have been referred to here and there as Mother Earth.

The Age of Complexity will require us to embrace femininity. Paradoxically, a more orderly world will emerge with the rise of the feminine. Too many people are simply too afraid to let that happen just yet. But they will have to learn.

Some imagine that disorder will follow in the absence of central control, when central control is the source of all the disorder they're beginning to see. Thus, excess masculinity drives too many human choices, which means too many people are willing to use or to accept authoritarian measures. After all, one is more likely to seek security in control when she is afraid. There is nothing wrong with the urge to control per se. We simply have to put it in its place. And that place is almost always local.

We have to restore balance. We have to think in terms of flow.

Eros Feminine and Thanatos Feminine are a needed corrective in a world currently dominated by Masculine Forces, but there is still a place for the Masculine in the rise of the Feminine.

In developing technological means to collaborate and cooperate, we must eschew the desire to design and plan as if society were a machine run by a controller. Instead, we have to create flow systems with a high degree of flexibility and liquidity. While Eros Masculine is not good at managing a complex system, it can be suitable for protocol design. The logical bases of computer code have a certain masculine quality —a forcefulness—that allows complexity to emerge. In other words, if the foundational rules are simple, logical, and stable— if x then y—then they are more likely to give rise to systems that flow more readily. Here, the masculine enables the feminine.

Healthy feminine enables the masculine, too, of course. Not only do most people thrive with a partner who cares for, nurtures, and believes in them—Eros Feminine—the organic patterns of living systems demand periods of rest and reflection that Thanatos Feminine embraces.

Indeed, it's easy to forget that Thanatos has healthy expressions, too, in both its Masculine and Feminine variants. Death. Ending. Absence. In polite company, it can be taboo to suggest such things. Few people, for example, have a healthy view of death. Most people feel ashamed when they secretly wish a severely demented parent would pass on. At some level, they know they are caring for what amounts to a husk of a self, but they live in a society of heroic measures. In their hearts they know there is little life here, but they endure the burdens. One wonders whether there is any dignity in this.

Just as our current political class seems overcome with the urge to control others, a cultural elite also seeks to control the aging process. In some areas, people have so much plastic surgery they appear to be wearing masks. Some find this macabre. Others see it as a status symbol. At some fundamental level, both perspectives reveal an unhealthy relationship with aging. Instead of accepting age as a fact of life, many hide, warehouse, or sublimate it. On the other hand, Thanatos gets expressed not in solemn rites or solid reasoning but rather in violent media that simulates killing and death. Even America's memorial days are more about potato salad and forgetting than about taking a moment to honor the dead. Contrast this with Mexico's *Día de los Muertos*, which manages to both venerate the dead and celebrate the living.

Though Thanatos is a kind of drive, we often seek to suppress or avoid it. The very thought of the *end* is depressing, and the very idea of ending oneself can be terrifying and a bit morbid. But not all death is to be avoided. Not all endings are bad. There might be no contradiction between raging against the dying of the light while accepting the end when it's near enough. Christians accept that Jesus had to die so that humanity could experience the living Christ and be saved. And in the Bhagavad Gita, Vishnu appears to Arjuna and offers a vision of the end that is also the start of another cycle.

In short, there can be good endings among the living and the dead. Think about someone leaving a company she is loyal to but the work no longer fulfills her. Think about living with a terminal illness in great pain compared to suffering's absence upon death or the sense of relief in knowing that a loved one no longer suffers.

Even the most ambitious among us have had to learn to accept failure, which is healthy in a case where one has done his best, but there is no way for a venture to continue. Sadly, too many cling to systems, relationships, or other arrangements well beyond their expiration date, usually out of obligation, tradition, or nostalgia.

Sometimes we have to find the courage to end something

actively, even a life. It's brave and good to have a suffering pet put down. That courage originates in Thanatos Masculine. Other times we must find the wisdom to *let go*. When a conscious decoupling is better for the children than staying together, this wisdom originates in Thanatos Feminine.

In the moments before letting go we can feel conflicted, which shows up as guilt, anxiety, or inner turmoil. But once we let go, relief can flow over us, signifying a healthy close. Letting go isn't always passive. It can be a conscious process to accept changing circumstances and adapt to them. In fact, if we are to thrive in the Age of Complexity, we must train ourselves to be adaptable. We begin by learning to balance the Four Forces within.

Just as aligning the Three Governors begins when looking inward, one balances the Four Forces in a similar fashion, but only after the Governors are aligned. It takes discipline and practice to sit in a space away from anger, fear, or anxiety. These emotions can overwhelm us. Indeed, most of us treat ourselves to a steady diet of anger, fear, and anxiety simply by reading the news. This keeps us in a state of indefinite imbalance. Our submission instinct can pull us to accept promises by the powerful to make those feelings go away. But they never go away. So, now we know we must confront our emotions and put them in their place. We must acclimate ourselves to operating in repose. Only here can balance be found.

It might seem strange, but learning to balance the Four Forces—first within, then out in the world—is the simplest and best path over time. Short-term acquiescence to imbalance almost always risks contributing to the arrival of Hell on Earth.

The Tree of Liberty, said Jefferson, must be refreshed with the blood of patriots and tyrants. So Thanatos Masculine speaks to us in words like "Revolution!" As a man, I certainly identify with that revolutionary fire. But we are living in different times. Thanatos Feminine says *let things go*. What America has become is not something Jefferson would recognize. What is needed, then, is not violent resistance or overthrow, but for a people to hold hands as we step into the black waters of the river at night. Let it envelop us, cleanse us, and shed us of all this rage for order.

Tomorrow we will be new.

5
MUTUALITY: FIVE DISRUPTIONS

> *It eats through just about every traditional concept, and leaves in its wake a revolutionized world-view, with most of the old landmarks still recognizable, but transformed in fundamental ways.*
> - Daniel Dennett, from *Darwin's Dangerous Idea*[1]

> *What cryptocurrency threatens is the very existence of the nation-state, which will have to pivot quite radically in order to survive the coming onslaught from the blockchain. The resulting institutional framework might look entirely alien once the dust has settled.*
> - Justin Goro, from "The Great Hard Fork"[2]

IN THE TIKAL region of northern Guatemala, a vast complex called *el Zotz* hides under thick growth. The complex includes temples, plazas, and thoroughfares once teeming with Maya. This once-great civilization eventually drifted into obscurity. Some say a mixture of drought and excessive foresting caused the inhabitants to abandon the city. Since its heyday a thousand years ago, the jungle has been unforgiving in its vengeance.[3]

A tidal wave of flora has swallowed the buildings, roads, and temples, turning mighty stone structures into mounds nearly indistinguishable from the surrounding landscape. Mother Nature can be relentless as she uncurls her snakes and unfurls her fronds. So the city has been returned to nature in unparalleled beauty and biodiversity. On the ground, of course, one can easily get tangled among the vines or bitten by insects —relentless forces of nature that once made it really tough to map the city. But in 2016, archaeologists began using laser-guided imaging technology to discover *el Zotz's* true extent, which is nothing short of breathtaking.

A LESSON IN THE LEAVES

Still, *el Zotz* is an object lesson. Intellectuals have turned collapses like the Maya's into Malthusian horror stories. And these stories are not entirely wrong. But a different interpretation recommends itself: Though humans can design big, amazing things, our plans and designs will eventually succumb to natural systems, which—though robust and orderly—are unplanned and undesigned. So, instead of seeing the jungle's revenge as nature defying human progress, we can see it as the victory of evolved systems over intelligent design.

But this doesn't mean there's no more room for human ingenuity.

As we enter the next era, we will start to mimic the patterns of natural systems so that our human systems are more resilient. And, indeed, we can use better protocol design to unleash a thousand systems that take their cues from Darwin. Nature, too, is about well-designed protocols, even though those protocols are not designed by a designer. DNA is catallactic. DNA is code. And in biology, code is law. At the macro scale, we get planetary ecosystems that include such wonders as the Great Barrier Reef and the rainforests of Tikal.

In the age of cryptocurrencies and smart contracts, the codebase is akin to DNA. With code, we can create systems within systems (within systems), which make up the layers of a technological and sociological stack. According to the codebase, these layers express different properties, which gives rise to a dizzying array of possibilities. These possibilities amount to five main areas of transformation in how human beings organize themselves. These are incommensurable with some of the older ways. In each case, therefore, we have an evolving technological ecosystem that threatens to replace the old order, which are the various temples to power. It turns out that like the temples to the Mayan gods, our modern temples require their own forms of blood sacrifice.

1. GOVERNANCE

The first temple to power is the Nation-State with its grand legislatures and executive palaces. Taxes supply blood for the gods in this temple. But a wave of technological solutions is allowing people new capabilities to self-govern.

The decentralized autonomous organization (DAO) is one such system, which can be instantiated in any number of groups using any number of consensus mechanisms. As more and more groups experiment with self-government using

DAOs, the more they'll see the power of programmable incentives and decentralized consensus. Indeed, the most promising feature of DAOs is not collective decision-making at scale. It is the built-in right of exit. The threat of defection looms over any system, which, unlike predatory states, has to provide value to keep members.

The temple gods are angry, though. Their very identity is wrapped up in the urge to control. They feed off our fears and leverage the extractive nature of the control structure itself. Power's priest class exists in a command hierarchy that offers them a sense of place, which they protect through increasingly illiberal means. And they worship in the Church of State on whose altar we will be sacrificed over and over again. This is the essence of Centralism. Instead of experimentation, variety, and choice in governance systems, they believe theirs is the One True Way.

The more Decentralists challenge their authority within a burgeoning ecosystem of cryptocurrency tokens, digital ledgers, and forking systems, the more draconian they become in their vain attempts to clearcut or burn our nascent rainforest.

2. FINANCE

The second temple to power is the Central Bank, with its esoteric symbols and shadowy meetings. Around them are supplicant banks, which serve as satraps in a system of private profit and socialized losses. All-seeing eyes and pyramidal structures are apt for a group that controls the sorcery of transmutation. In other words, these reverse alchemists need no longer turn gold into cheap alloys. They can magically debase the currency simply by adding zeros. Our blood sacrifice is inflation, which is nothing more than a tax on the powerless.

Decentralized finance, however, offers an alternative for the digital era, one that is transparent and disintermediates. With control and visibility of one's assets, anyone can gain exposure to global markets and alternative currencies with the properties she seeks. Decentralized finance offers an alternative to default systems whose existence has depended on the suppression of alternatives. DeFi grows harder and harder to suppress. In fact, the more anyone tries to regulate it, the more anti-fragile it becomes. As developer Justin Goro reminds us, cryptocurrency is a beast that evolves so that "the more the state clamps down, the better the evasive technology will get."

Unlike the legacy system, these alternatives offer financial services to anyone with an internet connection. By and large, these systems are owned and controlled by their users in a quasi-commons, not by middlemen. One can lend, borrow, long/short, earn interest, and more without custodians skimming off the top.

The powerful do not want ordinary people to escape crippling inflation or securities regulation. Financial institutions want us to operate within their matrix of go-betweens, brahmins, and fund managers, so we think their great pyramidal scheme is the only game in town. With DeFi, one can take out or pay off loans worth millions without the need for any lawyer, manager, or even personal identification. This is unprecedented in human history. The most powerful bankers in the world are understandably concerned, for their system is being threatened by underthrow.

3. ENTERPRISE

The third temple to power is the public corporation with its top-heavy management hierarchies and short-term incentives. Corporate gods extract blood sacrifices through the legal architecture of the corporation itself, which tends to rely on centuries-old organizational operating systems and static shareholder models.

A great power shift has arrived, which is transforming some public corporations into for-purpose partnerships with dynamic shareholder models.

- Instead of decisions flowing up and down chains of command through a layer of middle managers who create little value, enterprises are turning to self-management models like Holacracy—a framework for self-organization—that empower all and privilege no one. The mission is the boss.
- Instead of the traditional model that gives rise to a Taylorite class of scientific managers accountable to a disconnected cabal of shareholders, self-managed organizations also use rulesets that ensure decision-making authority gets distributed more broadly. In other words, those who have the most local knowledge and direct accountability make decisions within expertise niches.
- Instead of founders and investors gobbling up a greater share of proceeds, these forms disburse shares and dividends among all partners and colleagues from the start, according to the value of their contributions, including time and labor. Dynamic equity models slice up the pie according to principles encoded in their business agreements.

As more enterprises make these power shifts due to the problem of increased complexity, these new forms will come to predominate. And they point the way to a state of affairs that requires better rules, not better rulers: A world without bosses.

4. AID

The fourth temple to power is the Welfare State. Though connected to the first temple, it has its own inertia. In terms of its extractive nature, it might be the most voracious of all. This temple sits on a great moral high ground after all, from which the slings and arrows of sanctimony can be launched. That makes the Welfare State among the most difficult to reform or dislodge. People simply can't imagine that an underclass of relatively poor people can become anything more than liabilities to be managed by functionaries.

The Welfare State's very existence depends on wealth transfers that cause its recipients to become dependent. Massive constituencies become addicted to these transfers, which expands the very underclass the system was designed to help. The transfers create a perverse incentive structure in society, one that discourages those who produce more than they consume while encouraging those who consume more than they produce. This assessment might seem cold, but reality can be cold. A society whose authorities disburse aid by algorithm instead of targeted altruism creates terrible unintended effects. It also grows and entrenches a parasitic administrative class. Who will make sure all the boxes get ticked and the largesse dispensed? Those who will agitate to preserve the status quo.

Nearly a century ago, the Welfare State grew such that what had been a vast mutual-aid sector was eventually crowded out. In other words, people used to weave their own safety nets, but Welfare State functionaries made the need for this sector redundant. With the rise of cryptocurrencies and DAOs, not to mention ballooning debt and unfunded obligations, the prospects for renewing the mutual-aid sector grow brighter by the day.

5. DEFENSE

The fifth temple to power is the Military-Industrial Complex. Though connected to the first temple, it has its own inertia. And like the Welfare State, its appetite is insatiable. Its mission, once national defense, is now to expand an empire that extends around the earth. Instead of feeding on dependency, it feeds on war. Some argue that a global hegemon is good for peace, and yet what sort of peace can last when administered by an unholy alliance between those who profit from conflict and those whose *raison d'etre* is war? The blood sacrifice to the temple gods is not just tax, but literal blood.

President Eisenhower warned the world in his 1961 farewell address,

> In the councils of government, we must guard against the acquisition of unwarranted influence, whether sought or unsought, by the military-industrial complex. The potential for the disastrous rise of misplaced power exists and will persist.[4]

It's debatable whether the subsequent growth of this complex could have been avoided. But Eisenhower was right. His warning went unheeded.

Thus, the final of the Five Disruptions is called polycentric defense. This change vector might be the toughest, as most people simply can't imagine a world without a monolithic military brass orbited by contractors. The concern is that, without that monolith, there would be no defense at all. Even standard economics textbooks call defense a 'public good,' which means it's hard to supply the good and avoid free riders. So, no taxation, no defense. Today, the world's preeminent military power spends more than the next ten other major powers combined. And, in reality, free-riding is rampant. The system is also enormously wasteful.

One defense contractor charged taxpayers $4,361 for a drive pin that should cost $46.[5] Overcharging is common and is a predictable consequence of the fact that the military functions in no way like a normal market actor. It is a monopsony, a single market buyer, with incentives to expand. But there is precedent for a more competitive polycentric military that doesn't continue to bloat or degenerate, causing wars among smaller states. Consider the Hanseatic League.

Six hundred years ago, the Hanseatic League was a regional group of city-states that coordinated defense. This group held both economic and military sway in an area that went from Novgorod in northern Russia to trade zones near London. It lasted for about 500 years. The Hanseatic League established free trade among its members and created a navy and defense force to protect cargo. It succeeded in mostly eliminating pirates from the Baltic Sea.

Modern defense organizations are likely to use *unconventional* warfare because it's cheap and effective. One need only think of the effectiveness of the *mujahedeen* against the major powers in Afghanistan. Furthermore, if the incentives align around preserving peace rather than perpetuating war, each region would have a stronger incentive to help neighboring regions defend themselves before an enemy arrived on its shores. If the various defense centers got resources through more direct means—such as dominant assurance contracts—market forces would get injected into the defense ecosystem. Regional defense entrepreneurs would provide the people with what they need rather than providing politicians with whatever is politically expedient.

AS A FINAL NOTE, as more of the world puts its stores of value into the cloud, there is comparatively less value to be expropriated in meatspace. Bitcoin, the first and perhaps still the most resilient cryptocurrency, shows us the way. In short, authorities can invade a country to take over territory or steal its gold, but private keys live everywhere and nowhere. More and more value will live everywhere and nowhere, which means wars of appropriation are likely to decline as more economic energy gets stored in decentralized networks. More struggling jurisdictions will come to view expatriates as refugees of a dying hegemon.

Consider management consultant Matt Gilliland's transaction-costs model of underthrow. Gilliland writes, "When the perceived (risk/time-discounted) benefits of switching to an alternative exceed the perceived benefits of the status quo—including the perceived switching costs—people *will* switch to the alternative."

This formulation can be translated into steps:

1. Create overwhelming value in an alternative system.
2. Expose the diminishing benefits of the status-quo offering.
3. Change people's perceptions of the status quo system relative to that of the alternative.
4. Reduce switching costs.
5. Improve customer value within the alternative system.

Yes, there will be setbacks. And things are likely to get worse before they get better. But the Decentralist revolution is a djinn, and bitcoin's pseudonymous creator, Satoshi Nakamoto, opened the bottle in 2009.

6
MORALITY: SIX SPHERES

These great vows are universal, not limited by class, place, time or circumstance.
- Patanjali, from the Yoga Sutras[1]

I START with carbon because we start *as* carbon. Thanks to supernovae, star explosions that happened billions of years ago, we get to exist. These explosions sent carbon hurtling through space. The energy and matter that settled and accreted to make earth contained this critical constituent of life, so the self-organizing processes of life began with this simple element. At the risk of combining numerology with science, an atom of carbon has six protons and six neutrons in the nucleus, which get orbited by six electrons.

Without marking any biblical beasts, let's play around with the number six.

Carbon can come configured as a hexagon, which gives it important properties. For example, when scientists use lasers to arrange these hexagons in certain molecular architectures, it forms a fullerene. Fullerenes, named for Buckminster Fuller, are molecules shaped like soccer balls, only there is space inside these balls. What's striking about molecules, so configured, is that they are among the strongest materials on earth. Graphene (sheets), nanotubes (cylinders), and fullerenes (spheres) all make for durable materials due to the relationships among the hexagonal carbon atoms.

What if we could look at these amazing properties by analogy and imagine they can inform our human relationships? What in our normative universe can offer us strength and connection as Decentralists?

We are ready to explore the Six Spheres of moral practice. That means we sit squarely in the magisterium of ought, which we call right and wrong. The Six Spheres are *nonviolence, integrity, compassion, pluralism, stewardship, and rationality*. They are similar to what the ancients referred to as virtues, or features of excellent character. This approach is different from thinking about morality as duties derived from moral laws, though the Six Spheres are universal. Let the philosophers fight over justifying the Spheres, including metaethical questions. We can bypass those debates by making a bold proclamation:

If any given person (like you) wants to live in a world of relative peace, freedom, and abundance, then she ought to practice the six spheres to the most feasible extent and encourage others to do the same.

One might worry that the above "ought" is being derived from an "is" in a way that runs afoul of the is-ought problem. But ought, in this case, is instrumentally rational. That means it takes the if-then form: *If you want to achieve the goal of x, then you will do well to do y.* This form is different from *You ought to do y because y is good under some moral theory z,* or *it just feels right somehow.* That said, with conscious, continuous practice, the Six Spheres will take on the character of normativity as practiced virtue, complete with feedback loops. And that is good enough.

Because human beings have practiced the Six Spheres to varying degrees through time, we have gathered sufficient evidence that the Spheres work to the ends many of us seek.[2] We also know intuitively that excellent practitioners of the Spheres are those we regard as people of character, that is, people with whom we'd all prefer to interact. Then reciprocity recommends itself: People will want to interact with us if *we* practice the spheres, too.

Again, our goal is flourishing. Those who do not share the end of flourishing aren't locked in solidarity with us. So we must move on together in our practice without them.

1. NONVIOLENCE

The practice of nonviolence is not for the weak. Not only does it require strength that comes in self-discipline and self-control, but such control also begins in the heart and mind. Harmful words and acts begin as negative thoughts. So practice starts in rephrasing and reframing the internal chatter that keeps one company from moment to moment. In some respects, reflecting on one's innermost thoughts is the most challenging part of the practice, because we so often take our thoughts for granted. In other words, most of us aren't in the habit of reflecting on our thoughts, because it's easy to mistake our thoughts for reflection. Instead, though, we have to think about our thoughts. Because one's thoughts can seem to arise from nowhere, it's easier for harmful thoughts to leach into our words and deeds. Mastery of one's thoughts takes training.

> *Today I'm going to have an open mind about what I see. I will observe others with the mirror of empathy and be patient and circumspect in my response—that is if it's meaningful for me to respond at all.*

The practice is most important for those with whom we share our time. Yet it's often in being around those we love that we allow ourselves to fall into old habits. We should carry out the practice first for the ones we love.

"When you practice with others," writes spiritual teacher Thich Nhat Hahn, "it is much easier to obtain stability, joy, and freedom."[3] Maybe an ambitious goal for a parent is to create a certain culture of peace in the home. Creating a culture of peace starts with at least one person setting an example.

Hahn advises us to retreat to a monastery when we can. Otherwise, we must take the practice wherever we go. "This kind of life can be described," writes Hahn, "as monastic culture."[4] Most of us don't live near beautiful and contemplative places where monks can guide us. Some of us live with uncivilized children. That is why we have to remember that everywhere there is nature, there is a monastery. Taking walks among trees or grasses is enough to reset in contemplation. Otherwise, practice begins at home.

From there, the circle expands. But the practice of nonviolence is not enough.

In addition to *ahimsa*, we must also take on a mind-frame of nonviolent resistance against those who would harm or subject us. That includes agents of a state whose threat is comprehensive and systematic. Remember that when we get beyond the smiles, the elections, and the parades, politics terminate in the institutionalized threat of violence. Because Decentralism puts nonviolence at the center of all questions involving human relations, all of our ideas about politics—how it works, what it's for, and who should run it—are open to revision.

Just as *ahimsa* is the first of the Yamas among the yogis, nonviolence must become the presumption in resolving disputes and making laws, too. *Ahimsa* thus calls into question the legitimacy of the whole edifice of what we currently call society under coercive governments.

2. INTEGRITY

If nonviolence is the prime directive for the new order, the second is integrity. In other words, First, *Do no harm*. Then, *Be of your word*.

People use the word integrity in different ways, but in this context, it means honoring one's agreements to himself and others, committing to doing what he says he is going to do. Competing ephemera tempt us, so too many people think living in a world of smart devices absolves them of their responsibility to be on time, for example. But the wholesale transformation of society will only come about if more people can be trusted to keep their word. Society operates on people being able to rely on others.

Integrity, after all, has a law-like quality, like gravity or the forces that bind atoms together to make molecules. If people are going to organize themselves to achieve something, integrity is necessary for the group's ongoing performance. Integrity lapses introduce bugs in the system or breakdowns of interaction. Group performance suffers. Individual performance suffers too. Each setback affects other individuals who depend on the individual that comes before them in the performance chain. Therefore, practicing integrity as a universal should yield both individual and social benefits.

Failure to practice integrity means that some part of the whole is not operating according to expectations. Functionally, this amounts to inefficiency and breakdown, and of course, suffering follows.

This functionality isn't just for organizations. We can scale something like a Law of Integrity right up to society. We already have expectations of others we take for granted: We expect there to be some product at the market, but that depends on the production, packaging, logistics, and deliveries which came before. We expect there will be kind people to watch over our children while we work; we expect that if we have a deadline that depends on another colleague's work input, the colleague will do the work on time. And so on. The interdependent society operates almost entirely on people keeping their obligations. To the extent they do not, we start to see dissolution.

The yogis call these practices *satya*. They advise that, before one says anything, he asks himself: *Is this true? Is this necessary?* Satya includes being a person of one's word and one who listens closely and with discernment to others in seeking truth. Thus, to be *in integrity* means to endeavor to speak the truth, track the truth, and behave in a way that one's words, actions, and principles are all in alignment. This alignment includes not thinking one thing and then saying another. Integrity thus extends to those simulacra of self we put out into the world.

The practice would seem to begin with keeping the commitments one makes to those closest to him. But being honest with oneself is the genesis point. There is no way to enter the *sphere* of integrity through self-deception. Thus, when one fails to seek mastery in this sphere, things can fall apart around him. So, the foundation of being a person of integrity comes in the recognition, first, that one is only as good as his word, and then that he commits to the practice.

3. COMPASSION

When we think of compassion as a practice and not a bright moral rule, we can become attuned to myriad ways to apply it. Can we work out whether someone needs money or advice and emotional support? Can we help a being to die if it can't escape extreme suffering? Can we temper our sympathies for a neighbor who is morally lost?

Moral philosophers can point to the trailhead. But we all must practice within some set of circumstances with multiple confounding factors. Compassion is not an abstract rule we can apply. It is a way of seeing and a mode of being, which results in actions that *order reality. Tikkun Olam.*

For those who have ever had a small child, compassion comes a little more naturally. The little ones need us, and nurturing them comes easier than caring for a grown stranger. It can be harder to have compassion for adults who, as our elders used to say, "ought to know better." But we can follow the Sufis, who seek the divine light in everyone. Compassion starts with the disciple to look for that light even when it is difficult to see. Whether one believes Allah, God, or some animating essence is present in others, the practice of compassion works because she seeks value in others.

But compassion also means being attuned to others' hardship. The Sikhs practice *daya*, a form of compassion that involves *taking on the suffering of others*. It is deeper even than sympathy. One observes the stranger's pain and becomes touched by it, then he responds to the sufferer. He is moved to act with mercy and kindness. But *daya* does not require unreflective self-sacrifice. Nor does it require the machinations of politics, which are almost always an excuse for people to remove themselves from the discipline that compassion requires.

The practice of compassion, then, can be broken into the *affective*, the *deliberative*, and the *active*. That means practice starts with being attuned to the suffering of others, then one must ask oneself whether it is in his power to relieve someone else's suffering, and then ask how best to go about providing relief. After this deliberation, one takes action. The action could be a gift of assistance, money, advice, or emotional support. The point is that there are myriad ways compassion manifests itself in action, but people tend to neglect the importance of the deliberative stage.

4. PLURALISM

The practices of nonviolence and integrity are fundamental. But we need a third sphere, which arises from recognizing inevitable differences among us. It would seem that there is nothing new under the sun. After all, isn't toleration already a liberal value? Our familiar liberalism is too passive, a relatively bloodless and rules-oriented doctrine. To go deeper than toleration, we need to practice pluralism. By pluralism, I don't mean recognizing diversity in society, but rather the active practice of viewing differences in others through a lens of love and acceptance. It will take mastery to ascend to this level of practice, as it requires one to take on new habits of mind.

So what exactly does it mean to *practice* pluralism?

First, we can say what it doesn't mean. For example, pluralism isn't fixation with some group's victimhood status tallied on a cosmic scoreboard. Crude social theories of oppressor/oppressed are antithetical to pluralism. That's because, under such conceptions, people have to suspend their agency, rationality, and individuality. Some become mindless drones of an ideological monoculture in which diversity doesn't mean pluralism at all, but rather obeisance to a victimhood narrative.

The practice of the spheres serves the ends of mutual empowerment, not victimhood. Thus, pluralism in practice means seeking understanding, finding synthesis, and making peace. And that makes the practice of pluralism among the most difficult to master.

The first instinct for most ideologues is to dig in their heels and cling to a checklist of group-identity criteria. Identification with one's group too frequently comes before sound thinking. If someone else offers a perspective that is not on the checklist —or if that person belongs to an out-group—the ideologue is biased to look for what's *wrong* with that person's perspective. But what if we started looking first for what's *right*?

One who practices pluralism will have an open heart and mind, and she will not be so quick to retreat into tribal allegiances. Instead, she will discipline herself, looking for the alternative's best ideas and healthiest expressions. Eventually, she'll borrow from many different perspectives to build upon and strengthen her own. And then, she will *seek to synthesize the ideas*.

Take the example of poverty alleviation, and consider that three different groups have strong opinions on the matter:

- Progressives think people should emphasize care as a core value, and that entrepreneurship and markets are not enough to help society's least advantaged.
- Conservatives think there are right and wrong ways

to help the least advantaged, and those blanket welfare policies create dependency cycles that destroy communities.
- Libertarians think that entrepreneurship and markets do most of society's work in poverty alleviation, and people can carry out the rest through charity and civil society.

Many of us would look at these three claims and figure out which one is at the top of our in-group checklist. But the pluralist looks for what is valuable in each and weaves the strands together. In doing so, we borrow liberally from the Integral Theory practitioners' transcend-and-include approach.

And yet, this is not without paradox.

Eastern traditions speak of non-duality, which we can understand both in contemplation and meditation. In one respect, we must resist thinking of others as separate or *other*. Yet pluralism acknowledges each person's separateness. Therefore, we must reconcile the idea of sacred separateness with the fact of holism, that is, connection to the universe and each other.

Non-duality is challenging to articulate in cumbersome Western prose. Perhaps it is better to refer to the inner struggle Arjuna faced before going into battle in *The Bhagavad Gita*. The hundred who Arjuna is to slay are his cousins, all of whom symbolize the lower-order temptations and distractions which comprise the sum total of our embodied humanity. Of course, these hundred are under the command of the Blind King, who is Ego. Krishna's vision requires that Arjuna overcome these lower-order aspects of himself on the battlefield of his inner world so that he can understand his place in the cosmos. And with Krishna's driving the chariot, Arjuna can access just a little of that understanding, which will allow him to see that higher-order understanding is a triumph over Ego, but that everything that exists extends backward from the same cosmic source. Maybe the Gita is a kind of source code for recognizing one's singular place in the cosmology, but one interpreted as a unique manifestation of space-time's fabric. Krishna, Vishnu, and all other manifestations are aspects of the same mystery, partially revealed, unifying us all.

O Arjuna, in this world, all beings are born in utter ignorance due to the delusion of dualities (pairs of opposites, likes and dislikes), arising from desire and aversion.[5]

The paradox of pluralism is that understanding difference and diversity is a path to understanding a whole underlying truth. It connects all things. It *is* all things. So, for example, when we explore dualities such as creation and death, masculine and feminine, we regard patterns in the universe, of which we are part, expressed *through* us.

The practice of pluralism is about seeking a synthesis of perspectives, but it is also about seeking *unity*. In reconciling the paradox, philosopher Robert Nozick invites us to consider organic unity. The idea is that within any system, there is value in the balance of diversity and unity. Whether we're talking about art, science, or society, Nozick saw a pattern: *One can find value where unity and diversity are in balance.* In society, too much conformity means oppressed people, marching soldiers, and brutalist architecture as far as the eye can see. Too many stark differences, and one gets faction and unrest. According to Nozick, diversity and unity are mutually constraining. This kind of mutual constraint yields a sweet spot between rigid order and unruly chaos.

"Can we draw a curve of degree of organic unity with the two axes being degree of diversity and degree of unifiedness?"[6] asked Nozick in *Philosophical Explanations*. The diversity axis will constrain the unity axis and vice versa to achieve a kind of equilibrium. Apart from its simplicity, the beauty of Nozick's graph lies in its appeal to some intuitive sense of balance.

The dollar's dictum, *e pluribus unum* (out of many, one) is good, but so is *ex uno plures* (out of one, many). Integral thinkers are comfortable with the synthesis view of pluralism: Each person is unique and deserving of respect, but each is a manifestation of the same cosmic unity.

Why is pluralism in unity essential to our idea of society? When we are unified, we are probably at peace. But when we have peace, we each seek our own flourishing, which inevitably comes in different flavors. Pluralism means that people with varying conceptions of the good life can coexist while in pursuit. The practice of pluralism means that we balance our diversity with unity and attempt to weave our perspectives into a new tapestry. Getting a glimpse of that truth helps one see that monocultures are not always healthy, that experimentation is needed, and that reconciliation is possible.

Therefore, organizing society is not about finding a singular ideal to be crafted by masterminds. Instead, it is about acknowledging our differences, accepting them, and unleashing the creative forces that arise in the overlaps. Becoming a practitioner of pluralism does not come easily, and it starts with good old-fashioned toleration. In mastery, though, the practice means holding multiple values and perspectives in cognitive and affective juxtaposition. That takes discipline. So many of our reflexive responses work at odds with pluralism. It's rarely easy to understand and empathize with points of view that might go against the grain.

But therein lies a greater truth.

The hardest part is weaving together various perspectives into coherence while avoiding contradictions. To achieve coherence, we might have to shed fragments of those perspectives. These fragments can sometimes be pieces of our identities, insofar as our ideology or in-group identification shapes who we are. But no matter. That's what makes it hard. If we fail to achieve coherence, we end up with something that is not a greater truth at all, but instead, a muddle. And if we fail to seek greater truths, we will cling to fragments and remain in a state of disharmony.

5. STEWARDSHIP

The penultimate sphere is stewardship. Like the other practices, it too involves several dimensions that can be broken out and practiced in isolation. It's useful to think of stewardship as a cluster concept, mainly because it's easier to remember a word when getting started.

We enjoy relative plenty in today's world thanks to the liberals of the past. Our forebears made good rules and created wealth and know-how for us to inherit. It doesn't mean they created wealth in a perfect world, nor does it mean the world's material abundance is distributed according to anyone's ideals. It simply means that any given person alive today is likely to be wealthier than any given person at any other time in human history. We begin by honoring that fact.

Once we honor relative wealth, we must forget about ideologies grounded in envy and violence. Instead, we must focus on the stewardship sphere—whether we own a little or a lot. There is dignity to be found in stewardship, even if one has only modest means.

The old liberal rule of private property is a good rule, but is it sufficient? Private property is a precondition of trade and creates productive incentives compared with other forms of resource management. Like many rules, though, it is not enough. Owning property comes with tacit responsibilities and expectations, making ownership more than just a condition. It ought, like the other spheres, to be an active practice.

Stewardship involves moderation. Whether in Aristotle or the Yamas, it's good to adjust one's consumption habits or behavior to a reasonable level, avoiding extremes. Just because one has a lot of ice cream, for example, doesn't mean she needs to eat it all today. Just because one earned a lot of money doesn't mean she needs to live a life of ostentation. Moderation helps one protect the seed corn, which means protecting the means of investment and growth. It helps her appreciate scarcity before it arrives while taking a healthy attitude towards plenty, especially if she is tempted by it at every turn in advanced market economies.

Stewardship involves non-attachment. Whether in the Vedic traditions or Christian asceticism, non-attachment is a vital habit of mind in the sphere of stewardship. Why? One develops non-attachment to avoid privileging the destination over the journey, the salary over the effort, or the praise over the achievement. Non-attachment is a habit of recovering from feelings of loss but also a reminder that there is more to life than things. Goal-directed action is necessary as far as it goes, but the very nature of practice means losing oneself in habituated thought and action. She must honor the fact that resources are in her care and that they will be transferred into another's care if she exchanges them or when she dies. In other words, no one can cling to her possessions forever, and there will be times when she loses something important to her.

Stewardship involves leaving the world better than one found it. She should seek to improve any resources or offices in her charge. Then she should see to it these resources can improve the lives of others when they are no longer under her care. If she's not a good investor, her poor stewardship will be evident in time. Simply said, she will take losses. Investors who get rich from their investments are good stewards when the investment creates real value in society instead of just paper profits gained from political favor seeking. Those who have many possessions should otherwise keep them in good condition. And one who owns a modest plot of land should care for the fields, forests, and gardens. If one owns a business, she should seek to stay profitable and grow. If not she should sell to someone who can.

Stewardship involves sovereignty. With the development of token ecosystems accelerating, we have significant opportunities to be responsible for our assets. It used to be necessary to outsource most of that responsibility to financial institutions. But increasingly, we have the chance to manage our finances securely, without third-party intermediaries who command considerable sums for their intermediation. As we become more sovereign in controlling our resources, we will become more mindful in our consumption and giving.

Ownership is mere possession. Stewardship is a practice. If each of us continues to improve and grow the resources in our care, we will improve the world around us. Once we start to reframe ownership as stewardship, we will begin to see improvement in the world and in ourselves.

6. RATIONALITY

The final sphere of the six is rationality. Woe unto those who think rationality is a relic of the Enlightenment. Instead, it is a faculty that humans evolved to survive together in harsh conditions, and it provides us with cognitive abilities for achieving our ends. Like the other Spheres, we must practice rationality—that is, being rational. And just as with the other Spheres, rationality involves more than paying lip service to a single word. It includes other nested concepts necessary for us to continue together in cooperation, but in the end, one can't cooperate without tracking truth. Despite the playful verbosity of postmodernism or the mysterious phenomena of the quantum realm, we must continue to labor under the assumption that we have all to understand the features of our universe to navigate it. Rationality becomes the bedrock of all the secular magisteria, including science and law.

Justification. Rationality is first the process of mining good reasons for holding a belief or working towards an objective in a certain way. In the absence of justification, there is randomness. While applying randomness over rational justification can be useful in certain narrow circumstances—such as solving complex problems with evolutionary algorithms—justification is essential to human decision-making. That way, others can understand our rationale, which is particularly important for deliberation or collaboration. One vital feature of justification is evidence for making a claim.

Evidence. When offering justification for a belief or behavior, we ought to provide some sign indicating the claim *tracks truth*. In the absence of evidence, there is only faith or logic. And faith is primarily useful in the magisterium of religion. Such is not to argue that articles of faith never appear in science, as indeed they do. Instead, it is to say that faith is not the primary mode of truth tracking. Instead, we need the world to offer clues, which get mined in observation and recorded as data.

Critical thinking. With some evidence-based justification in hand, one usually needs logic and reason to organize the rationale so that others can readily understand and their understanding leads to no contradiction or fallacy. Eschewing contradiction and fallacy involves critical thinking, which is the deliberate application of logical analysis or clear reasoning. Critical thinking thus requires intellectual discipline, which forms a coherent set of beliefs that indicate some claim is likely to be true.

Bayesian thinking. Even though we might have evidence and feel certain, we need an effective way to deal with uncertainty. The Bayesian view of probability relates to the degree of one's belief. Given incomplete knowledge, we can get an idea about the plausibility of holding some view. Bayesian thinking is based on the idea that one can know more as more information comes in and becomes integrated. We can use these methods to combine results from different experiments, for example, as the data are often scarce, noisy, or biased. Some might view the adjusting probabilities of Bayesian thinking as a limitation of the rationale. Instead, it is a way to understand the world around us using imperfect information and limited knowledge while admitting that sometimes truth-claims needn't be binary.

Fallacy and bias. Much of our contemporary discourse is plagued by fallacy and bias. Indeed, sometimes people consciously employ biased or fallacious reasoning in order to persuade others or reinforce the beliefs of those in their in-group. Good discourse norms must be distinguished from rhetorical tactics, but these tactics do not serve the ends of truth tracking. After all, biases can be natural tendencies to think a certain way, in that one's brain, as it were, plays tricks on him. Fallacies are patterns of illogic that lead one to preoccupy himself with matters that are not relevant to the inquiry, or that stir up emotions that can interfere with gaining clarity.

It might be strange to some readers to think of rationality as a moral sphere. Consider, though, that these spheres stand outside of time. In other words, no matter where one is situated in history, truth tracking is always vital to human flourishing, which we define as happiness, harmony, and prosperity. Rationality is the toolset of truth tracking.

THE SIX OFFENSES

Sometimes good practice in the Six Spheres includes knowing what to avoid. The Six Spheres of moral practice have vicious mirrors, the Six Offenses.

Violence is nonviolence's vicious mirror. Of course, it is to be avoided as nonviolence is foundational to the Consensual Society. That doesn't mean one should not defend herself. It means we proscribe the *initiation* of violence in every sphere and at every scale, practicing nonviolence in thought, word, and deed.

Corruption is integrity's vicious mirror, and it can take many forms. In essence, though, corruption is actions based on untruth, abandonment of one's principles, or consciously failing to honor one's commitments—all for personal gain.

Callousness is compassion's vicious mirror, which means a cold indifference or sense of cruelty in the face of another's suffering. If we are to create a benevolent society, we must become attuned to suffering and practice compassion.

Monomania is pluralism's vicious mirror. One sets about zealously to impose the One True Way upon everyone else. Of course, there is no One True Way for different people living in different contexts, all of whom have different life plans.

Negligence is stewardship's vicious mirror. Whether we fail to attend to our possessions or take responsibility for our offices, negligence can be offensive to the project of taking care of the world around us, from one's garden to our global ecosystems.

Casuistry is rationality's vicious mirror. Usually, this vice is employed to mislead or deceive, but sometimes it can be a careless lapse into fallacy or a failure to acknowledge one's biases. If we are to track truth together and improve our collective intelligence, we must avoid casuistry.

IN SUBSEQUENT CHAPTERS, we will discuss values and insights that spring up in the context of trying to understand our wider moral universe as we develop in our complexity. But the Six Spheres are, in a sense, eternal. That is, the Six Spheres are as good a set of moral practices as one can imagine for most any human context—whether on the prehistoric savannah or staring down from a modern skyscraper. Contrarian philosophers will busy themselves with exceptions or counterexamples. But in the end, If any given person wants to live in a world of relative peace, freedom, and abundance, then she ought to practice the Six Spheres to the greatest feasible extent and encourage others to do the same. The aggregate effect of such practices among more people will allow our children and grandchildren to inherit a moral universe that improves the world.

7
MINDFULNESS: SEVEN RITUALS

Between stimulus and response there is a space. In that space is our power to choose our response. In our response lies our growth and our freedom.[1]
- Viktor Frankl, from *Man's Search for Meaning*

EACH DAY of the week offers an opportunity to be mindful. That might mean practicing the Spheres, clearing the head, focusing the mind, or otherwise returning our thoughts to our doctrine, even briefly. The Seven Rituals are here to guide you.

To some, this might seem strange, occult even. But consider that occult just means hidden knowledge. The Seven Rituals and their associated arcana reveal knowledge you have deep within yourself. The hidden knowledge our rituals reveal will guide us in our daily commitments to realizing the Consensual Society.

The point of these Rituals is not to give you the impression of staring into the bowels of a religion. First and foremost, the

Rituals are instruments of transformation. After all, *We shape our tools and then our tools shape us. We shape our rules and then our rules shape us.* Rituals function as a way to reshape ourselves despite the matrix of incentives left to us by the old order. If we are to expand our sovereignty and be prepared for the social singularity, we will have to do everything in our power to transform.

Powerful forces will cause us to doubt ourselves. We might lose heart. We might weaken and be dragged back into the well-worn grooves of the old order. In this way, the Seven Rituals can help Decentralism compete with other well-developed doctrines, including the Church of State. Centralism has its rituals, after all. So we shall have ours.

Now, if the goal is to expand our sovereignty, shouldn't we be looking around ourselves to see just how? That comes later. First, we have to look inward. And we have to *practice* looking inward.

THE SPACE

Holocaust survivor and psychologist Viktor Frankl left us with powerful words. As ritual involves repetition, allow me to repeat the epigraph:

"Between stimulus and response there is a space. In that space is our power to choose our response. In our response lies our growth and our freedom."

This single insight provides a basis for Frankl's therapeutic practice and offers foundational wisdom for our daily practices. All practice requires you to begin in the Space. In other words, the best way to expand your sovereignty is first to expand the Space.

Remember also that Frankl developed logotherapy on the idea that human beings continuously search for meaning, where meaning is perhaps the most sacred form of happiness. In our search for meaning, however, we confront innumerable decisions. We make many such decisions in an uncontrolled manner. But first, in finding the Space, and then in choosing our response, we practice deeper self-possession. In time, self-possession, which comes even before the practice of the Six Spheres, can allow one to heal herself.

This is the basis of our agency, and indeed our sovereignty. As Buddhist monk Phap Dung reminds us,

> We see the mind like a house, so if your house is on fire, you need to take care of the fire, not to go look for the person that made the fire. Take care of those emotions first; it's the priority. Because anything that comes from a place of fear and anxiety and anger will only make the fire worse. Come back and find a place of calm and peace to cool the flame of emotion down.[2]

Returning to this insight periodically prompts us to *choose our response*. That takes discipline. But once it's developed, this power is nothing less than mind control. Devote any opportunity simply to sit more consciously in the Space before taking action. After a while, you'll learn to operate in the Space when doing so matters most. The Seven Rituals are designed to help you expand the Space.

1. PRAYER

Mondays start the week for most people. A new cycle begins, which often comes with dread. On Mondays, then, we require confidence, determination, and resilience. We remind ourselves periodically that we have a mission, and we must rededicate ourselves to it.

Forking Paths: A Prayer

I am sovereign.
When I practice peace,
I create a light,
Which radiates outward,
As ripples on a pond.
Neither dictates from one,
Nor ballots from many,
Shall take our peace
Or dim our light.
It is yours and
It is mine.
Build the Society, and
In harmony entwine.
Once together,
We can commit,
Bound by the governed's consent.
Once we've seen our commitments through,
I'm free to go, as are you.
We're sovereign,
So let us work,
In common interests,
In common need.
Our bond is strong,
Is that enough
To plant the community's seed?
With Reason's light
And an exit right,
We might linger here as friends.

If paths diverge,
We hold Six Spheres,
In pursuit of different ends.
For only in peace
Might we live,
And live well,
To start anew, and
On forking paths continue.

---

2. ACTS

Tuesday is for an act, but not just any act. An act can be one of kindness, bravery, or demonstrated commitment. But the general framework is as follows:

Today, I will do something against the grain.

What does it mean to go against the grain? It can be simple. Suppose you are in the habit of putting off unpleasant tasks till the end of the day. At this point, you are tired or unfocused. Next time, instead of procrastinating, go *against the grain*. Put the unpleasant task first, then reward yourself with more fulfilling activities for the rest of the day.

Can you help a neighbor despite being busy? Can you find the courage to try something new? More than doing unpleasant things, acts of this sort help you grow through perceived limitations. Maybe you know you should find the courage to start writing something you have had in your mind. Tuesdays can also be dedicated to that ritual, but you have to start by putting down some words.

The discerning reader might wonder how the acts relate functionally to Decentralism. Among many answers, the most fundamental is that *we must train ourselves to do difficult things*. And difficult things must start somewhere. Another answer is that the Age of Complexity requires constant change. Having the courage to change can be as simple as saying to yourself: *Just do it.* That requires you to practice sitting in The Space, even if it's to gather your courage. The Acts will help you become accustomed to being versatile so that you can adapt to novelty and change.

3. REPETITION

Wednesdays can be stressful, and stress can be a headwind. Because repetition requires you to focus your attention, it can have a calming effect on your mind and body. Just as a rocking motion soothes a child, repetition can soothe the mind. But to repeat a phrase is not just an utterance. It's something you do to set an intention as you strive to become.

In the Vedic traditions, people use mantras to help them meditate or focus. Repeating a sound, word, or phrase can be rhythmic, which helps align the head, heart, and gut, or what we have called the Three Governors. Repetition also allows the phrase's meaning to penetrate other competing thoughts and mental chatter. But most importantly, repeating is a form of spiritual annealing. *The more you exercise it, the stronger you become.*

Repetition isn't woo. There is deep psychological resonance in the ritual. Even a simple word like *cup* automatically creates a form in your mind, even if it's just written once on the page. It is difficult, if not impossible, for that word to be devoid of form. Now imagine vocalizing that word over and over. When you repeat an utterance, *you* become connected to both the name and its form, which creates new pathways to transformation.

Entrepreneur Tarun Nimmagadda put the matter in a tidy formula and shared it with me:

The Power Law of Compounding Habits
$$\Delta \text{ You} = \text{Habits}^{\wedge \text{ frequency}}$$

One can write this more prosaically as *Ceteris paribus, Your rate of change is the habits you choose compounded to the frequency of the habit you practice.* Of course, younger people have greater neuroplasticity, but the benefits of practice accrue to us until we die.

To what should one direct her practice?

Because the Six Spheres lie at the center of our moral universe as Decentalists, imagine them as illuminated spheres. They swirl, then settle, in the mind's eye. Each sphere has an associated phrase. Which one is relevant today? Linger on that Sphere and repeat its phrase, which should make the others disappear and the primary sphere come into focus.

- I will radiate peace today, harming no one.
- I will be true to myself and others.
- I will be more attuned to others' suffering.
- I will better care for what is in my sphere of control.
- I will honor differences in others as part of the great tapestry of being.
- I will weigh evidence, avoid doublespeak, and seek the truth.

Mantras for emotional *control* help us to avoid becoming victims of envy, anger, or fear.

- Envy is uninvited; my value stands.
- Anger is a toxin in me, so I wash it away.
- Fear does me no good, so I release it in three out-breaths. (Breathe deeply three times.)

Mantras for emotional *channeling* can also help us *redirect* negative energy for success.

- Envy impels me to improve.
- Anger is fire to anneal my resolve.
- Fear makes my courage possible.

For success, Mantras help us to avoid getting trapped behind obstacles or falling into pits.

- I will persuade my enemies in time.
- My failures are lessons learned.
- My weaknesses are paths to improvement.
- I flow as water toward the sea.

Mantras for perspective help us realize that we are both great and small, whatever the world's problems or our own.

- Life's vastness fills me with wonder.
- I revere the tiniest miracles around me.
- I am part of a Great Unfolding.

Mantras for balancing the Four Forces should be obvious.

- Exert control.
- End it now.
- Let things flow.
- Let things go.

Choosing a mantra must begin in the Space, or at least helps one find it.

Finally, repeating phrases can help you keep our resolve in the face of overwhelming Centralist power.

- As long as I injure no one, I am justified.
- I possess the Keys.
- Experts should show me options I might not see, not make decisions for me.
- Consent is the foundation.
- Concentrated political power is order's illusion.

Of course, one can always simply vocalize the OM, which reminds us we are part of the cycles of birth and death that are part of the cosmic mystery. OM animates those who wish to be free to seek meaning.

4. WALKING

Thursdays can be for walking, but not just any walking. Even daily walkers should take Thursdays for a contemplative walk. Walking with your hands joined behind you facilitates contemplation. Going outside offers opportunities to connect with nature, to be grateful for your existence, and to wonder at the bountiful universe.

5. SYMBOLS

Let Fridays be for symbols. Arrange these in your environment, or choose one to wear as a modest adornment. These can be good for Saturdays, too, as we'll see, but on Fridays, the symbols are for you. The visual-symbolic modality is powerful, so let us take advantage of that fact.

The Eye. In Decentralism, we poach the Eye of Providence. The Eye represents "The Grand Architect of the Universe" for the Freemasons. According to the higher orders of the Eight Stages in Decentralism, though, the universe is not architected at all, but rather emergent. Variations on this symbol should thus be free of any pyramidal structures. However, the Eye persists as a symbol of our inner eye, which represents both our vision, our pursuit of mission, and our ability to find wisdom in the Space.

The Hexagram. Six points equidistant, configured in a circle, serve as nodes, each of which connects to every other node using lines. The 'nodes'—small circles—represent the Six Spheres of moral practice. Some will opt to use six Eyes to stand in for each node. This symbolizes our inner eye as it regards each of the Six Spheres. Of course, interconnected nodes in this configuration also represent decentralization.

The Wrapped Fist. This symbol can be an image or a gesture. Thus, when Decentralists congregate privately, we can show respect by bowing the head slightly and wrapping the fist to show our commitment to nonviolence (though not pacifism). In other words, the fist-wrapping rite calls to mind the restraint of violent power by wisdom.

The Elements. Recall the Four Forces (Eros Masculine, Thanatos Masculine, Eros Feminine, and Thanatos Feminine) can be represented as earth, fire, water, and air. However, four alternative symbols will work in lieu of the elemental symbols: insects. The scarab (earth), the moth (fire), the dragonfly (water), and the butterfly (air) are alternatives that call to mind both the elements and *six legs*, which symbolize grounding in the Six Spheres. Some will find it necessary to select which symbol is appropriate for channeling a Force, primarily when one seeks balance.

Eyes. Multiple interconnected Eyes can be configured to represent Decentralists in solidarity. They can also represent the mutually acknowledged sacredness of persons. In this symbolism, the connected Eyes evoke the idea that other *selves* are apertures into a greater Self or interconnected Set of Selves unified in an unfolding cosmic story. Under this construal, the idea of Providence is not of a distant, supernatural entity who controls the universe at his whim. Instead, it is the totality of consciousness, however broadly and mysteriously it extends *from* or *as* the cosmos.

Tree/River. Vascularization is everywhere in the natural world. To the extent that a system creates channels and conduits that make flow possible, that system "lives" or persists in time. Such systems are not *alive* in the same way that a cat or a tree is alive, but they still have a life. We want to symbolize the Law of Flow with a tree or a river basin. For example, squinting at a tree or flying high above a river basin offers more or less the same type of vascular patterns. These are flow patterns. Or as I write in *After Collapse,*

> In the Amazon, far below the rainforest canopy, a network of roots stabilizes a thick trunk. Mirroring the branches and twigs among the leaves above, the roots below split into smaller roots, which split into yet smaller roots, extending outward to absorb water. All that water gets stored in the tree's cells.
>
> A few miles away, a mighty river rushes. The river carries watercraft and fish, a few large and many small, inexorably toward a delta. What feeds the great river are smaller rivers, Apurimac and Mantaro, then tributaries, which are fed by streams, which are fed by brooks, which are fed by sources high in the Peruvian Andes.
>
> Navigating the river early in the morning, an old woman goes fishing. Her body contains a system of veins and arteries that carry blood, enriched or depleted, to nourish every cell in her body. Likewise, her brain and limbs are animated by information

signals within a network of nerves. These signals have to be processed by an organ of fractal complexity, or the old woman will be unable to navigate much less fish.

Such is the Law of Flow.

The Nautilus. The creature's distinct spiral pattern frequently appears in the natural world. There seems to be something fundamental in the Fibonacci sequence or the Golden Ratio, which are mathematical ways of describing its distinctive form. For us, this 500 million-year-old creature symbolizes time, evolution, and emergence due to its status as a living fossil. Its chambered shell, which has not changed over millennia, is perfectly evolved for deep-water buoyancy.

Stones and Fire. Our forebears once sat around a fire. Stones arranged in a circle around the fire kept it from burning out of control. When fire symbolizes the sacred, the circle of stones represents a separation between the sacred and the profane. When fire symbolizes knowledge, the stones represent a boundary—humility or circumspection—as knowledge can confer godlike powers.

6. OUTREACH

Saturdays are for engaging others in good discourse, specifically around our doctrine. As opposed to evangelism, how about outreach?

Recall that as practitioners of nonviolence, we have to be persuasive while abstaining from coercion: fist in palm. That means the goal of Decentralism is not conversion so much as it is persuading others about, well, persuasion as the primary mechanism of change. If the vision is of a Consensual Society, we have to be the proverbial change we want to see. And that starts with outreach, which can be a simple conversation.

If you are lacking an entry-point for outreach, a thought experiment might help:

If you could wave a magic wand and eliminate all violence or threats of violence from the world, would you do it?

Your counterpart is likely to say *yes*, *no*, or *I'm not sure*. From there, "Why?" seems appropriate, and further dialog is likely to unfold quite naturally. Some will want to hear more about your motivations. In that case, you can respond by saying that answers to such questions reveal something about her, which is indubitable. *Imagine a universe where even if someone thought about making someone worse off in some way, the magic of the wand would simply prevent them from initiating the harm, like an invisible force field.* Hopefully, from there, a conversation can flow.

Decentralism is a doctrine with its own beauty and elegance. It requires no evangelists with missions of mass conversion. Instead, it can be a surrogate for religions lost, or, more importantly, an alternative to the Church of State, which has gobbled up generations of lost children. Our doctrine simply requires a hearing. It is as giving some a flame, wick to wick. That's because Decentralism's primary mode of transmission is optimism, not fear.

7. LITURGY

Sunday is for liturgy, because most of the time, Sunday is a day of rest or reflection. If this is not true for you, you can make any day your Sunday. The point is an opportunity for public worship. But when we get together, what exactly are we worshiping?

One another.

Worship is the deepest reverence one can give to a sacred entity. We hold as doctrine that other persons are sacred. Too frequently, though, our instinct is to treat others as if they are something *other* than sacred. Perhaps we treat them as if their aspirations are unimportant or as if they were mere means to some ideological end. However, turning our ascriptions of holiness onto one another reminds us we are all manifestations of a cosmic unfolding.

Is it odd that one might draw from the trappings of organized religion at all? Is this a doctrine or dogma? Whatever Decentralism is to you, remember that many of the major world's religions have outlived empires. Such is not to argue that no instantiations of any religion have been harmful. We simply want to reinforce that certain features of religion offer something prose cannot: a way of tapping into deeply human centers that we have called the Three Governors. Indeed, there is tremendous power in getting people together in a room to recite something in synchrony. Liturgy of this form can tap into powerful aspects of our consciousness.

Saying so would seem to betray a kind of nakedly instrumental justification for liturgy, but utility is just one side of the coin. It's not enough to bind people together with contracts and hand-shakes. We must symbolize and ritualize our recurring commitments because, in so doing, they take on greater meaning, *felt* meaning. Whether in a Sunday liturgy or anything else, doing ritual together awakens a sense of connection and purpose that reading and reflection alone cannot. We experience something deeper, something irreducibly social, that fills the abstractions of doctrine with life.

The Seven Rituals, including the liturgy, are modes of practice designed to shore up our basic philosophical perspectives and patterns. We rewire our brains and reset our convictions. If nothing else, rituals keep our mission front of mind. Otherwise, the liturgy lets us connect more deeply with each other and to the sublime. One cannot simply read about the sublime, after all. One must experience it.

If you already have a religion or set of spiritual practices, none of this is intended to replace those. Our practices are for people who need them. For now, then, the following is a framework for Sunday gatherings. This calendar corresponds to the seasons. Each item under the seasons represents a single week out of fifty-two and offers participants an opportunity meaningfully to reflect on a particular aspect of life.

Liturgical Calendar

Spring	Summer	Fall	Winter
Creativity	Knowledge	Wisdom	Introspection
Vision	Wonder	Altruism	Entropy
Endeavor	Evolution	Community	Trauma
Novelty	Reason	Meditation	Failure
Beauty	Journey	Integration	Death
Emergence	Prosperity	Change	Posterity
Courage	Friendship	Meaning	Resilience
Identity	Enterprise	Mentorship	Respect
Holism	Excellence	Commitment	Aging
Development	Consciousness	Communication	Memory
Play	Happiness	Order	Posterity
Love	Complexity	Sublimity	Impermanence
Nurturing	Pluralism	Conflict	Divinity

Notice that all of the items are universals. In other words, each word represents a category common to everyone, alien to no one. We will be diverse in our interpretations but unified in our commitment to reflection.

SCRIPTURE AND SKEPTICISM

Ritual is powerful. It gives people opportunities to shore up their fundamental commitments as individuals and groups. Almost by definition, Decentralism has no great figurehead. Therefore, we must create opportunities for observance that have their own gravity. Decentralists with the soaring oratory of an MLK or the patient resolve of a Gandhi are always welcome, of course. For now, our objective is to offer insights people can use to animate a living doctrine, which is the work of a simple scribe. Once our doctrine animates more than a few souls, it will begin to evolve—for better or worse.

"A ritual is the enactment of a myth," writes Joseph Campbell.

> And, by participating in the ritual, you are participating in the myth. And since myth is a projection of the depth wisdom of the psyche, by participating in a ritual, participating in the myth, you are being, as it were, put in accord with that wisdom, which is the wisdom that is inherent within you anyhow.[3]

One can hear the tutting from those who have a religion or the pshaws from those who do not. The religious might think of this as an effort to pluck esoterica from their faiths for sinful purposes. The rationalists might view this as an effort to pull them from their comfortable agnosticism into some kind of cult. The truth is probably somewhere in between. If you think there is a better way to fill the voids of morality and meaning in modern man, bring forth your amphoras.

8
MATURATION: EIGHT STAGES

And he dreamed, and behold a ladder set up on the earth, and the top of it reached to heaven; and behold the angels of God ascending and descending on it.
- Genesis 28: 10-19[1]

Visible in unmistakable clarity and devastating detail is man's failure to be what he might be and his misuse of his world. This revelation causes him to leap out in search of a way of life and system of values which will enable him to be more than he has been.
- Clare Graves, from *The Never Ending Quest*[2]

IN LOOKING at our developmental journeys, we discover patterns.[3] Maybe we impose these patterns on societies, or perhaps they reflect the rhythms of homo sapiens unfolding in complexity. Whatever means determine them, we can understand various stages as part of our social reality. First, we see the Eight Stages of life. Then we accept them. Then we sacralize them.

Each Stage comes with a bundle of values and insights that can help us thrive in various life contexts. As the Eight Stages are vital to understanding humanity's journey to Decentralism, we honor them as distinct means of adapting to life's vicissitudes.

Thus, from each distinct cluster of values and insights we form an Order.

Each Order is a sacred subset of the whole. While we must face the fact that there is a stepwise aspect to development, which corresponds roughly to degrees of cognitive and social complexity, the totality of the orders does not amount to a formal hierarchy. No one order is superior to another. As we suggest above, each order should be thought of as sovereign because it is in unique life conditions that each Stage arises. Such makes the whole set of Stages non-linear and non-hierarchical, a living system with indistinct contours and porous borders. Some have described the Stages as a spiral, others simply as stages, but we appeal to the work of giants on whose shoulders we stand.

1. ORDER OF THE NAKED: SURVIVAL, SENSATION, AND SELF-CONCEPT

You are helpless. Your circumstances present you with brutal binaries. Eat or starve. Drink or wither. Live or die. At this stage, you are more or less a tropistic being, an advanced cluster of cells changing with the surrounding stimuli. You are human, but only barely. You are becoming. In times of severe privation, you will return to the values of this stage, which are bare and basic, just like you. For now, you are a mewling blob of reflexes and possibility.

Crying or cooing are instincts, just like mama's *there-theres*. She overcomes the gravity of sleep to feed you and burp you. Founts of fermented spit-up tell her you're full for now. Were it not for her or some parental figure to nurture you, there would be no higher-stage entity to appreciate this Stage. In other words, you don't care. You are wholly unable to reflect on such insights, much less show gratitude for them. Maybe you reward your caregivers with cuteness or some other joy of parenting, which nature has programmed in them to enjoy to compensate for the burdens you represent.

Your values, such as they are, are simple: *Do what is in your limited means to survive.* Most of those means are programmed into you by an ancient code which exists in every cell. Experience does not write itself onto your brain in the manner of etching a blank slate. Instead, sensory data impinge upon a complex array of molecules. Those molecules will execute as your genes instruct, but the genes will express themselves according to some of those worldly stimuli. You are thus the product of nature and nurture tangled in a miraculous dance.

As you continue to be shaped by forces largely out of your control, something mysterious arises between the forces of nature and nurture to assert itself. You become *aware*. Then you start to form memories. Then you become aware of *yourself*. Along the way to self-awareness, you become more acutely aware of those around you, too. Where before your experience had all been an inchoate blur, your sentience is crisp. Now in high resolution, you experience the world—whether in the pain of want, the pleasure of satiety, or the bliss of mother's love. Dynamic interchanges between you and those around you shape you, and you shape them, but you are not infinitely malleable. Your genes demand limits and form contours that make up your unique attributes. By the by, the process of interpersonal shaping shuttles you into the next stage.

2. ORDER OF THE MOON: CLAN, ANCESTORS, AND NATURE

Welcome to the clan. Our communal ties are strong. Our blood ties are stronger. In the harsh milieu of the steppe or the forest, we have to look out for each other. Without interdependency, we would die. Some hunt so that all can have meat and fat. Others gather so that all can have berries and tubers. Still others settle disputes and offer wisdom to the group, especially the elders who have seen many cycles. For our clan to survive in harsh conditions we must share, which means hoarding is detrimental to our survival. If we do not share in life, we will undoubtedly share in death.

We sit together around the fire, which is sacred. The firestones circle a space into which only our ancestors can go. Fire is a doorway to the next life among the creatures, trees, and lichen. We regale one another with stories of ancestors, daemons, and animal familiars. After the children drift off to sleep, we configure ourselves using the moon's phases and the position of the stars. We used to hear wolves circling our camp in the night, but we drew in a couple with the marrow of broken elk bones. Now they protect us. The elders say one of those wolves is your great-great-grandmother, and she guards you when you sleep.

The elders have enormous power. One we call Soaring Spirit. When he closes his eyes and goes into a trance, his soul floats above him and interacts with the dead. From their communion, Soaring Spirit relates messages to us, which help us to heal. Sometimes, Soaring Spirit delivers bad omens or sees death. But we must listen, for we are all fated to become protector wolves, swooping hawks, or guardian stones. Until we die, we live in harmony with everything around us, even the spiders, snakes, and scorpions. For they, too, are part of the cycles.

But life here is not easy. Resources are getting scarcer. Today we went out for a hunt. Instead of finding food, we encountered others like us. Only they bore odd hair, skin, and markings. They commune with different spirits. We suspect they have begun to kill our game and take our women. Therefore, we must learn to fight as a unit.

3. ORDER OF THE FIST: COURAGE, HONOR, AND EGOISM

You bring honor to your clan with every strike at the enemy. Every parry and cut is a step towards mastery that your kin shall inherit. If you ever feel fear creep into your heart, you must knock it down by beating your breast and riling your brethren —for you are mighty, mightier than the elements! If the rain comes, it will cleanse you and fill your waterskin. If a fire blazes, you will roast the haunches of a goat! If the wind comes, you will curse your enemies and laugh with the gods as your beard and braid flutter in the breeze.

Hear that? Is that a battle cry just over the horizon? That is your calling. Today is your day.

Your tunic is blood-soaked! The battle is won. You dance with your kin around decomposing heads on pikes, Xs for eyes, delivered to the clan from the battlefield. Our vanquished foes took too much from us, so we must not let them pass into the nether realms just yet. We shall have our turn punishing their souls, just as we punished their bodies out on the moors. The fighting is over, for now. Still, their vengeful cousins await yonder in the West. Soon their balls will descend, and they will come thirsty for blood.

For your bravery, you are a hero. You have trophies and war spoils, which mark your fitness as protector and provider. Young women offer themselves to you as you bask in this glory. Maybe one of them will bear you a son so you can train him as your father taught you: to fight in swift, coordinated action.

Because you have brought glory to the clan, you can indulge today. You should feast tomorrow, too, for the day after that, you may die. You should never fear death, though. As long as you die in battle, your death is glorious. The clan will sing about you. If you never get to die in battle, you will live to watch your sons become great warriors, and your daughters raise great warriors. So eat! Drink! And save some seed for the wailing wives of the damned!

You have grey in your beard now, but you are chieftain. Your enemies are beaten back or dead. Just as you achieve supremacy, a loud voice strikes you with a message: *Your bravery and unquestioned command of the men means your clan has expanded. But the clan is also falling into disarray. Some shirk. Others loaf, pilfer or fuck when they should be working, training, or planting. Disease outbreaks are more frequent. Babies are being born bastards. If your clan is to continue to expand, you must learn to rule. That means you must establish an administrative kingdom.*

4. ORDER OF THE PYRAMID: GOD, MORALITY, AND AUTHORITY

Learn humility and kneel before the voice who has delivered this Divine Insight. For without order, chaos will overcome our people. If our enemies don't soon find our fighters flabby and undisciplined, they will eventually find them dead from disease or famine. We are thus commanded to establish order.

As all things must, the Moral Order radiates down from God. The sovereign is God's imperfect embodiment on earth. His decisions are absolute. Edicts flow down a nexus of control in a great chain of being. In this configuration, each must know his place. One comes with a telos, which connects to a plan that, though mysterious, is magnificent. To execute His divine Designs, the king must bend to the Almighty, the governors must bend to the king, the magistrates must bend to the governors, the highborn must bend to the magistrates, the lowborn must bend to the highborn, and the animals must bend to the lowborn.

To maintain this Holy Order, everyone must sacrifice to the Almighty, which begins with obedience. Such sacrifices include taxes of gold or grain to his protectors. In addition to material sacrifices, we must make spiritual sacrifices, too, such as carrying guilt. To avoid spiritual pollution, embrace virtue, avoid vice, and observe cleansing rituals using water, oil, and smoke. Sinners must be punished or shamed publicly, with the severity of the punishment matching the extent of the sin. Bearing witness to a sentence helps the people to realign, reminding them of their place in building a kingdom that God will favor above all others.

Those with means have a duty to sacrifice some treasure: Alms go to the poor. Tithes go to the priests. Taxes go to the king. The poor cannot toil without victuals. The temples are not resplendent without riches. And it is the sovereign's duty to fortify his kingdom and to dispense largesse. Viewed from without, the temple ascends, reminding us that God is all-powerful. Viewed from within, the temple reveals glorious details, symbolizing the prophet's words, the soul's composition, and the Lord's manifestations. When the wretched gather near the temple door, with pock-marked faces and filthy outstretched hands, we must remember that they too are God's children. The temple is for everyone.

When everything in the kingdom is working according to God's Design, we must expand into the realms of the unclean. Soldiers march into the hinterlands not as raiders but as crusaders. Those subsumed by the Moral Order must be civilized, from blasphemy to piety. Otherwise, they will continue to harass us at the borders, or worse, worship beasts and false gods. We must slay and discard the unburied corpses of the unrepentant, so their souls wander as ghosts until something most foul pushes up from the ground and spirits them off to Hell.

Any deviation from kingly fiat or scriptural commandment opens a gate to demonic forces who seek to raze the kingdom and feast upon our souls. So we must never deviate. Thus the moral order eats the weary world around it, transforming the barbaric and benighted into the good and the true.

Yet amid the orderly administration of God's design on earth, there is an unsettling paradox: Certain men with open eyes claim to see the law-like nature of God's design in the firmament. They melt glass and fashion it into shapes, which lets them see beyond the horizon, charting astral bodies and heavenly orbs. Planetary patterns appear to them as clicking gears, despite the proclamations of their king or the revelations of the priests. Would God bypass the most faithful in his flock by revealing his Laws directly to low-born eyes? Or is such cleverness a form of sin?

5. ORDER OF THE SUN: SCIENCE, COMMERCE, AND REASON

In addition to the technical feats of lowborn men, merchants with vision and attunement to their desires are busy making plenty on the High Street. The butcher cuts for the baker, and the baker kneads for the butcher. The brewer needs to eat, and the baker loves his ale. The banker keeps tabs on them all. So as each trucks, barters, and trades, something miraculous yet undesigned springs from them as they toil away to enrich themselves. Prosperity bursts forth and compounds, such that our city shines among cities. Surely there is good in this.

In the light of Reason, two magisteria become pronounced: science and commerce. Suddenly, streets and alleyways pulse with life and color. Music spills out from theaters with their players primed for the wealthy as the lutes, flutes, and stringed gourds of happy buskers keep the lowborn cheery as they nurse their ales. Some have pockets heavy with coins, which makes the highborn green. The philosophers hustle to the agora, newly awakened in their knowledge. They question the hoary ways of faith and obeisance.

Linear logic and cautionary tales about fallacy replace many beloved myths. Practitioners of this way of thinking are obsessed with understanding what is *real* in the world around them, not to mention how that reality works. They resist postulating anything without evidence for its existence. But not without controversy. Some think all truth claims, even those of math and logic, must be tested in the crucible of experience. Others believe such truths are born within us, waiting for reason's light to shine on them.

In the overlaps between these more pronounced magisteria, we find innovation. As more and more people find they have the freedom to tinker and the incentive to profit, they develop technological recipes which they can learn, adapt, and apply in myriad ways to create a Great Barrier Reef of possibility. In this ecology, one discovers a fundamental law of human interaction: where there is production, there is competition and specialization; where there is trade, there is mutual benefit, all of which gives rise to exponential wealth creation.

But is a world of transactions and testable hypotheses the end of history? Or is this linear world fraught with problems? As we create wealth, we discover unhealthy excesses in greed, corruption, and environmental degradation. Some end up with great riches, while others survive on little. Despite the enormous progress and prosperity created under the commercial system, we must adopt new values and appreciate new insights to curb its excesses.

6. ORDER OF THE LEAF: ENVIRONMENT, CONSENSUS, AND EQUALITY

Spaceship earth is our home. The only feasible alternative is a rusty planet with no atmosphere, bathed in every moment by radiation. Yet greedy industrialists are racing to colonize this inhospitable place instead of righting the wrongs against our planet. Rather than restoring the earth's natural ecology, some industrialists seek to terraform planets that are not fit for human habitation. We should weep for our Mother Earth and cry out against the inequality that exists in the name of science and commerce.

It's not just our environment that needs repair. We are also spiritually deprived due to rampant materialism which creates radical inequality. To rectify this, we need to restore balance to our economic systems by sharing the surpluses of human progress with the least advantaged. The existence of billionaires should be viewed as a failure by the greedy and dogmatic to unite in the people's demands for social justice, which require a higher degree of wealth equality.

In the age of hypercapitalism, too many people focus on acquisition. This creates a kind of spiritual anemia that can only be cured by people coming together to connect more deeply as a community. Eventually, that community can extend to everyone as we become a global village. In such a state, we will learn how to manage our precious commons. To avoid the frictions associated with returning to a more communal lifestyle, we must adopt means of finding consensus and creating harmony. Let every voice be heard. To the extent that there is social unrest, we must include those at the margins of society. We must struggle alongside them, for they were put there by a lower order's powerful oppressors.

While we are comfortable dispensing with the idea of truth as something to be discovered in the world instead of experienced by the subject, we are not giving up on ideal justice. We can abandon Truth for cultural relativism while remembering that a story told enough times becomes our truth. That's how we march through the institutions. That's how we install ourselves in hierarchies once reserved from the privileged. And that's how we assume control on behalf of the oppressed and marginalized who are yearning for equity.

Yet, in such zealous commitments, will we start to channel some of the former Stages' unhealthier aspects while forgetting their healthier insights? If we do, we will come to feel hopeless, even nihilistic. Are we, in our sanctimony, seeking to create another moral hierarchy within a dangerous administrative state? Have we forgotten that the very forces that generate abundance might be employed to help the natural world and lift the poor simultaneously?

7. ORDER OF THE NAUTILUS: INTEGRATION, EMERGENCE, AND COMPLEXITY

You have made a quantum leap in consciousness. The first thing you see clearly, that you could not before, is the value of integrating insights of the prior Stages. Not only does each have value in the context of specific historical life conditions, but each has value in modern life. Not only must we relate to others in different Orders, but we must appreciate the subtle circumstances that require us to *see* and *be* in the different Orders from time to time. Those who have not yet ascended will interpret your agile movement among the Stages as wickedness or wizardry. But it will be necessary for those who have ascended to become fluent in each Order's tongue, including this one.

Apart from the need to integrate diverse values, one of the primary insights of this Stage is the ability to parse two different types of systems: those which we design and those which emerge. The latter, emergent systems, are the hallmark of this Stage. Members of this Order focus on protocol design instead of system design, for the former gives rise to systems that are beyond our ability to design.

Evolution and emergence work together to form complex systems governed more by rules and less by men. Indeed, complex systems exhibit stunning degrees of order, despite our urge to control. And this order, in turn, is essential for understanding the development of life on Earth. Therefore, one discovers the sweet spot between flexibility and function, which means we must learn to guard against the urge to design and plan everything. This urge can manifest itself as unhealthy technocracy, that is, authoritarian versions of so-called 'systems thinking.'

Add to integration and emergence the ability to live

comfortably in the flux and flow of open systems. Life is bountiful in its diversity, and there seems to be a close connection between that very complexity and living a flourishing life. We know, however, that diversity and complexity can be threatening to those in prior stages, so we must, in our mastery, develop heuristics for those still ascending. That way, they can handle the onrushing change.

Mastery in this stage also leads to limits. We already alluded to the limitations of systems thinking, which too frequently lapses into technocratic overreach. One can also flock to others who appear to have ascended but, once embroiled, can engage in an obscurantist arms race whose watchwords are *nuance* and *meta*. On other occasions, one grows weary of interacting with the other Orders on their terms, and she can feel like a chameleon. One day, though, she experiences a breakthrough of sorts. It involves uncovering new mysteries while investigating the old ones. It consists in wondering at the dynamics of the whole.

8. ORDER OF THE LOTUS: HOLISM, PARADOX, AND INEFFABILITY

Suddenly we can see the relationships between wholes and parts, parts and wholes in ever-shifting complex patterns. That does not mean we can design or control such systems any more than we can design or control the dynamic intricacies of Earth's ecology. Systems affect subsystems, and subsystems affect systems. Everything is generative, iterative, and regenerative, at least on this pale blue dot.

We begin to see not only how higher-order properties can be reduced to simpler constituents, but we can also see how one *cannot* reduce such properties. Replace linear arrows of causation with probabilities and paradoxical cycling phenomena. We are forced to abandon our crude deterministic outlook and stare straight into the cosmic mystery. One answer reveals a thousand questions.

On a subatomic scale, familiar rules seem not to apply. When we observe the photon, it appears as though it goes left in virtue of our observation, rather than that we simply watch it go left. Click out many orders of magnitude. When we see the black hole's behavior, it requires us to revise and relativize. What's on the other 'side' of the black hole? Another dimension? Another universe? Time and space aren't distinct categories but rather dual aspects of the same underlying phenomenon. Spacetime curves and stretches in the presence of supermassive structures.

Categories of reason break down, particularly when we push the boundaries of science into the theoretical. Yet unobservable entities live in theory, often for decades, until we develop ways to infer their existence in the absence of direct observation. In this Order, philosophy and science make strange bedfellows. Maybe our investigations at the edge reawaken our sense of the mystical, or maybe we have a peak experience.

Diving into the mystery does not require us to abandon rationality but rather to expand our conception of it. Such expansion ought to include holding two or more contradictory ideas in juxtaposition without lapsing into incoherence. Our task is to figure out how to reconcile or synthesize these ideas using lateral or non-linear thinking. This form of cognition is difficult and rare—impossible for some—but can give rise to an understanding greater than the sum of parts.

Some explorers of the self, referred to sometimes as psychonauts, will have direct experience of conscious states that prompt us to reconcile strange forms of understanding with the more familiar forms. These include the *ineffable* and the *noetic*. Ineffable knowledge means difficult or impossible to put into words, which can cause one to doubt that it is knowledge. Noetic knowledge is directly revealed, which means it is radically subjective. The revelatory nature of such experiences leaves one with a sense of a cosmic source delivering the insights. One such insight is often that all things are fundamentally connected, which can be trivially true and construed as hippie talk. But a deeper sense of connection, gained through meditation or peak experience, confers meaning. Happy residues of such an experience can be patience, wonder, and humility.

Few have dared to wonder whether another Stage is waiting to be born. Such a stage will arise from changing life conditions if it emerges at all. I suspect innovation will begin to dissolve so many of the categories we are used to being fixed. For example, what does it mean to be human? To what extent can we fundamentally alter ourselves, change our genetic source code, or merge our neurophysiology with AI?

IN EXPLORING THE STAGES, we must do so with the utmost humility. Each Order becomes expressed within certain life conditions. Some of those life conditions include individual limits to one's cognitive abilities or capabilities. Some worry that natural constraints that prevent some people from ascending create an unbearable natural hierarchy.

"Stage theory... Is BS", writes author Nora Bateson. "Always was. And it is colonial as hell. Sorry, but that has got to go."

The trouble is, it can't go. Whether we view the Stages more as a heuristic than as a hyper-accurate description of humanity or ignore them altogether – some variation on increased psycho-social complexity will operate in our reality.

Instead of colonialism and unbearable hierarchies, I propose the Stages make up a *heterarchy*, which means members can be ordered in any number of ways along many different dimensions.

In other respects, differences create a *holarchy*, meaning there is no absolute base or apex. Relationships relate wholes to parts in different ways according to a given environment. As with a fractal, the patterns evident at one level of description can be similar to those at another. Thus, the values of a superordinate Stage might be somewhat useless in the life conditions of a subordinate Stage. That is, until one makes the quantum leap to the Order of the Nautilus and the Order of the Lotus.

Those who ascend to the Order of the Nautilus do so, like others, by their newfound values and views on the world. But their quantum leap involves a newfound ability to jump from Order to Order (system to system) as needed. They are not only able to see where each Order fits into the Whole of Orders, but they become conversant across orders. Nodding to Jonathan Haidt, they learn to move flexibly among different moral matrices as the situation requires. For example, they might see the value of saying "yessir" or "no, ma'am" to their elders, as would be familiar in the Order of the Pyramid. Or they might see that those steeped in a more toxic version of the Order of the Leaf will no longer be able to appreciate that the decentralized processes established in the Order the Sun. These can be better at solving social problems than deferring to the pieties of social justice, or Green shibboleths.

One might worry that this quantum transition confers special insights that will allow those who have ascended to take advantage of those still on their lower-order journeys. Maybe it does. All bets are off in the absence of the Six Spheres, which run orthogonally to the Eight Stages as soon as moral dealing emerges in humans. Happily, one of the hallmarks of the ascended two orders is a greater sense of humility and wonder. That is, we come to appreciate our human limitations as we operate in the Age of Complexity.

By this point, we have figured out that complexity requires Decentralism. Thus, Decentralism's time has come.

9
MARKETS: NINE PRINCIPLES

The curious task of economics is to demonstrate to men how little they really know about what they imagine they can design.
  - F. A. Hayek, from *The Fatal Conceit*

IF WE ARE to develop a comprehensive Decentralism, we cannot overlook economics. Because economic science can take us to disciplinary depths rather quickly, we should set out a simple set of economic Principles. These double as institutional design heuristics. Indeed, the Nine Principles allow us to see through a lot of the fictions that pass for analysis these days, particularly as the dark spells being cast on ordinary people are based on inscrutable mathematics or models that hide legerdemain or omit critical aspects of reality. At the very least, we can go forth into the world armed with Principles that, when abandoned, indicate a theoretical house of cards. So equipped, we can begin to apply the economic way of thinking.

1. VALUE

All value is subjective.

Through the ages, some of the world's finest minds have built whole theories on the idea that value is objective. They attempt to use, say, labor and capital inputs to derive its value. But the cost of the inputs doesn't simply add up to create a product's value. From Adam Smith to any number of contemporary economic thinkers, the idea of objective value supplies a foundational premise for whole theories. Remove that foundation, and the rest of the theory usually collapses. As it should. Consider this simple illustration:

Two different manufacturers make two different shirts, but each produces the shirts using the same number of labor hours, materials, and dyes. In other words, the inputs are exactly the same. The only difference is that on one shirt there is a picture of Karl Marx; on the other, a picture of Carl Menger.

There is no such thing as intrinsic value, according to Menger. And he's right. Despite the fact that Menger was right about the nature of value, and Marx wrong, we can use Mengerian insights to predict that then, as now, Marx is more widely known and more fashionable. So the Marx shirt is likely to fetch a higher auction price. The material inputs are simply immaterial to the question of value. Why? Value is always in the eye of the beholder. If circumstances change, one's valuation might change. For example, if a beloved celebrity were to wipe her brow on the Menger shirt, the market value of the Menger shirt might change. Indeed, it cost the celebrity only sweat, so if the market value of the shirt went up by a factor of ten, we wouldn't be able to argue that the celebrity or the shirt manufacturer exploited anyone's labor. It would simply be the case that *someone* was willing to pay for a celebrity-sweat-soaked Carl Menger shirt. The costs of the inputs are wholly irrelevant to market valuation, that is, whether consumers desire the outputs.

What about a basic resource such as water? Surely that is objectively valuable due to our universal need to hydrate. I may want to take that bottle of water and put it to my parched lips to survive. You may want to load your squirt gun. I'd pay a hundred dollars for that water in the right circumstances, for example after a jog in the desert. You might only be willing to give a buck. Maybe we can agree that the circumstances of time and place can prompt us to value things differently.

But matters run deeper. We are different, you and me—*on the inside*. We are likely to value any given thing differently, even in identical circumstances.

> *Jack sprat could eat no fat,*
> *His wife could eat no lean.*
> *So betwixt them both, you see,*
> *They licked the platter clean.*

Despite the cries of economists with all manner of letters, there will never be any such thing as intrinsic value. There might be intersubjective agreement about value, but value does not inhere in things. It never can. It never will. Value is a feature of our subjectivity. And the relevant unit of analysis is individual choice.

2. EXCHANGE

Voluntary exchange is likely to make both parties better off.

Far from being a problem, whole economies operate according to people's subjective valuations. Consider a circumstance in which there is a double coincidence of wants: If you like my apples more than your oranges, and I like your oranges more than I like my apples, we should probably make a trade. Each of us is likely to be better off if we do. This formulation is deceptively simple. In the absence of force, fraud, or bad information, exchange occurs in lawlike fashion when two parties believe they will be better off than if they do nothing. Of course, anyone can get buyer's remorse, but that is not relevant to the Principle, *Exchange is proof of perceived mutual benefit.*

Even in circumstances where there is no production, exchange alone can improve the economy. Imagine that one day various items fell like manna from above. People would snap up items as quickly as possible to prevent others from doing so. Under this first 'distribution,' people are not likely to be all that satisfied, especially if they can see what items others are snatching up. Manna items fall at random, after all. But when people start to trade, more and more find satisfaction. Indeed, the more we can all see of the market, the more likely any given person will satisfy her wants—at least if she has something to trade.

3. RULES

Economies operate according to institutional rules, and some rules are better than others.

No complex economy can exist without rules, whether explicit or implicit. And rules are human ascriptions. That does not mean that all rules are created equal. It means that economies require a facilitation function for economic actors who will likely never meet, and who may not even speak the same language. The rules are, in a manner of speaking, a *lingua franca*. They have instrumental value.

Political economists refer specifically to institutional rules. In other words, what is the matrix of rules on which this or that economy operates? How do those rules shape our behavior through the incentives they create?

Consider three basic rules upon which advanced economies run: *property*, *prices*, and *profit and loss*:

Property is a set of rules about who owns what. Without some institution of private property, even if only implicit, there can be no exchange and therefore no mutual benefit. Private property also creates strong incentives for resource stewardship, whether in conservation or entrepreneurship. If no one owns some valued resource, people will race to exploit it. We call this situation a tragedy of the commons. Overconsumption is part and parcel of these problems. One rule is to allow common-pool resources, somehow, to pass from an unowned state to an owned state to prevent overconsumption and encourage economic activity. Homesteading, public auctions, and other methods can aid in this transition. On the other hand, some political economists see value in a managed commons. In this scenario, the property remains in the commons but gets stewarded by locals operating according to evolved community rules. According to Nobel laureate Elinor Ostrom, managed commons are notoriously difficult to maintain and scale, which is why she warns against large-scale or bureaucratic commons management.

Prices. Market actors can set prices through their actions, or authorities can set prices through their edicts. But history has shown that the latter creates a series of distortions and difficulties. Because economies are complex and constantly changing, they cannot be known by a single mind or committee of minds. No one can precisely allocate resources among competing wants, needs, and subjective valuations. Prices are "knowledge wrapped in an incentive."[1] If, according to your valuation, the price is too high, you might seek a substitute or do without the good or service. If you find the price is too low, you might be an arbitrageur who buys more of the good or service to resell in scarcer markets. Between supply and demand, market actors tend towards equilibrium, which is referred to as market clearing. Prices coordinate this process in a way that no authorities can.

Profit and loss. All organizations, from coops to megacorporations, ought to exist within a profit and loss system. Simply put, if revenues do not flow to the organization, it is almost always an indication that the organization is valuable to no one, and that its very existence wastes resources. Interventions, whether bailouts or subsidies, paper over the signals that give us a better idea about an organization's true value. Outside a profit and loss system, this type of value cannot otherwise be rationally determined. Whenever we stray from such a system, the institutions will attract pirates and predators with promises of paper profits. In other words, not all profit is the same. Paper profits that flow from favor-seeking behavior such as subsidies do not reflect market value. Only those organizations that can internalize all costs, including environmental harms, and freely attract customer or investor income *over costs* ought to exist. And this includes providers of governance services in the Consensual Society.

There are myriad other institutional rules from which to choose. But as innovators experiment with new forms of governance, they must introduce rules that are more likely to benefit any given system member, however unequally. Rules ought to regularize behavior instead of determining outcomes, just as a traffic rule to *drive on the right* creates predictable patterns without determining our destinations. And as I suggest, governance systems that don't satisfy member desires will lose those members. Lost members mean lost revenue. And lost revenue ends in failure. This is the way of things in healthy economies, just as it is in healthy ecosystems. We forget this lesson at our peril.

4. MONEY

Anything that serves as a medium of exchange, unit of account, and a store of value is money, primarily, though money can include myriad secondary properties.

Another inconvenient truth is that, under most circumstances, a double coincidence of wants is nigh impossible to find. Villagers can barter, of course, but that severely limits the range of wants and needs a given villager can satisfy. The ancients solved this problem long ago with the introduction of money.

The principle is that money has specific properties that make it useful as a medium of exchange, a unit of account, and a store of value. Ancient peoples used seashells and shiny stones before using precious metals or banknotes. Indeed, money has historically been an emergent phenomenon, which is hard for some people to appreciate. In other words, no one planned or designed the use of money any more than they planned or designed the language they use to communicate.

Powerful authorities realized they could extend their power by issuing fiat currencies, where fiat simply means *I deem it so*. The Romans used precious metals, for example. Still, the Emperors found that each time a coin passed through the treasury, they could adulterate the coin and return it to circulation, having taken some amount of gold, say, out of the *nummus aureus* for themselves. Roman authorities debased the currency through the centuries, which caused persistent inflation. Despite technocratic fever dreams, inflation is a tax that is, on aggregate, harmful to the many, including and especially the poor. Today, central banks don't debase coins. They simply print more notes or add more zeroes.

There are nine distinct properties of money that, in most circumstances, one might like to instantiate in a given currency: scarcity, durability, portability, divisibility, recognizability, ease of storage, fungibility, difficulty counterfeiting, and usage. With the introduction of cryptocurrencies, though, innovators imagine all manner of other properties that might be useful in various contexts, such as stability. These new currencies and their associated properties show us that there is no *one true money*, but myriad monies that give us the properties we need in various circumstances according to our subjective valuations of their utility. One great benefit of these innovations is that decentralized digital currencies are difficult, if not impossible, to debase or control. We can look forward to an era in which our monies become far less corruptible by central banks and their coterie of supplicants, which we affectionately call Wall Street. Happily, the functions bankers once served might soon be served by coders.

5. ENTREPRENEURSHIP

Entrepreneurs are more likely to create value for any given person when their ventures compete, internalize their costs, and earn revenue above those costs in a marketplace free of coercion.

Value creators behave in generative and prosocial ways because they have specific gifts, some acquired, others inborn. They make money when they take risks and apply their talents in a way that *customers* are willing to reward them. Yet, not everyone sees things this way. So it's essential to explain why entrepreneurship must be among the market's Nine Principles.

There are three basic types of entrepreneurs: *arbitrageurs*, *innovators*, and *organizers*. And of course, truly great entrepreneurs express all three of these personality types:

An *arbitrageur* is an investor who tries to profit from market inefficiencies she perceives, especially when she thinks others can't see them. These inefficiencies can relate to any aspect of the market, including prices, dividends, or regulations. The most typical form of arbitrage is price. *Apples sell for x dollars per pound here. I can find similar apples and sell them for y dollars per pound and still make a profit.* The arbitrageur is attuned to these opportunities, and she gets a reward for rectifying the inefficiency.

Innovators are entrepreneurs who see ways to do something novel. If the novelty creates a product or service that is better, faster, or cheaper, then she will be rewarded with profits from those eager to avail themselves of the novel value. Innovators quite literally create new recipes that make the world a better place.

Finally, *organizers* serve a valuable function. This type of entrepreneur knows how to configure talent, resources, and management systems to create customer value. Startup founders have to figure out how to put the pieces together to overcome the gravity of liftoff. Seasoned executives have to run complicated operations or implement self-management protocols that allow their firms to grow and evolve. Neither is possible without both a clear purpose and a profit motive. In this way, purpose and profit become two sides of the same coin.

The principle of entrepreneurship says that anyone who creates value, reflected in revenues over costs, is a kind of entrepreneur. Despite long-standing views of entrepreneurs as exploiters, most entrepreneurs simply possess relevant gifts that help them sustainably create value. And entrepreneurs need not be CEO types who are lonely at the top. Some entrepreneurs join forces in self-managed organizations. Others, such as social entrepreneurs, find ways to achieve a social mission, but they too depend on income, whether in sales or donations.

Every product or service you enjoy, including the words on this page, is made possible by an entrepreneur. But one must be careful not to overstate matters. Entrepreneurs who are successful because they rig the political game to their advantage are no better than entrepreneurs who simply fail. A real entrepreneur's failure comes at his and his investors' expense. The rent-seeker is playing a negative-sum game where lost value comes at *your* expense.[2] For example, if a company would not exist but for taxpayer subsidies, then that company is destroying value. While rent seekers might be talented, their activity is not prosocial. We exclude them from our formulation because a preponderance of rent-seekers will ruin a society in time. After all, to extract rents is not really to create value.

The Principle of Entrepreneurship, which says healthy economies are composed of people creating value, has a corollary called Strong's Law, from educational entrepreneur, Michael Strong:

"*Ceteris paribus*," writes Strong, "properly structured free enterprise always results over time in higher quality, lower cost, and more customized products and services."[3]

A society composed of real entrepreneurs will give rise to

untold prosperity. And for that, they deserve a little bit of respect and a lot more room.

6. INEQUALITY

Healthy economies are inherently unequal.

The Inequality Principle is simple: Inequality, under normal conditions, is a feature of the economy, not a bug. If inequality results from political entrepreneurs locked in an unholy alliance with the political class, that is destructive to society. But if inequality is a natural consequence of differential contributions of insight, work, risk-taking, and capital contribution, we should expect nothing else. In that case, the Law of Flow predicts the economy will look like any other living system: we will see life's scaling laws manifested as large, medium, and small. That means scaling laws are not equal.

Imagine you're walking in a rainforest. It's rich with life—verdant, beautiful, and diverse. When you look up, you notice something striking. A few giant mahogany trees dominate the forest. Their canopy covers almost everything. After reflecting some on these trees —you give them reverence. They are towering, majestic, and sustain life for a bewildering array of other plants and animals. Yet, those smaller plants and animals help sustain the trees, too.

But nothing is equal in the forest.

The mahogany trees soak up so much of the forest's resources, including sunlight, soil, water, and air. You decide the mahogany trees are *hoarding* resources. Their biomass takes up nearly 80 percent of the forest ecosystem. It's just not fair that they should have so much while the smaller flora and fauna have so little. Thinking about this inequality, you wonder if it would be better to cut, cull, or pair back some larger trees.

Soon you come upon a group of tribesmen. They share some magic with you, which they say allows you to "talk to the forest." Being an open-minded sort, you heat up some root with water and make tea from the root. Then, you plunge deeper into the jungle with your heart burdened with a message of rectitude.

"Hey monkey," you say, wondering if the root works.

"Why must the mahogany trees take up so much sun, water, and light?"

To your surprise, the capuchin turns his head and replies: "Without them we'd have no boughs on which to stand, nor fruit, nor shelter from the storm."

"It seems unfair, though," you return. "Without you little ones, the mahogany seeds would have no fertilizer. Their seeds would not so easily find a place for their saplings to take root."

The capuchin says, "This is true."

A tree frog overhears. "Yes, if we depend on each other so, why aren't we bigger and the trees smaller? Why shouldn't we have more of the resources?"

The capuchin thinks for a moment. "One thing is certain. If we cut them down to our size, we'll be living in an empty field."

Frog says, "I couldn't live in an empty field."

"Nor could I," says the capuchin, turning back to you. "I wonder, traveler. Is it in the forest's nature that the trees are large and we are smaller and more numerous? That they control the water and the light? And would the rainforest be this plentiful without these giants here?"

The atavistic desire for equal economic outcomes is a fetish manifested by paleolithic brains. When humans lived in small clans with little refrigeration and severe scarcity, equal sharing meant clan survival. But outside of family and charity, a clan ethos has no place in advanced economies. If one is concerned about the least advantaged, she can always practice compassion. In compassion, she will come to appreciate the distinction between humane concerns about poverty and envy-based feelings about inequality. The former emphasizes means that lift up the poor. The latter emphasizes means to confiscate wealth. Never mind that people have significant moral objections to confiscation. From an economic point of view, confiscating wealth creates no value. It merely transfers it.

To reiterate, the Principle of Inequality implies that economies operate according to proportionality. Any reward that accrues to one ought to be tied as closely as possible to their contribution to a profitable endeavor, and flow from sovereign choices, not choices by sovereigns. Institutional reform that minimizes compulsory transfers—whether from poor to rich (cronyism) or rich to poor (welfare)—will not create an equal society. Such reform will, however, create a more harmonious society. By removing mechanisms through which groups antagonize one another, the rich can become more compassionate, the middle classes to save more of their seed corn, and the poor to seek mutual aid and upward mobility.

7. ECOSYSTEM

Economies are most like dynamic ecosystems, not static machines —because economies evolve.

Let's extend our biological metaphor into a general understanding of *economies as ecosystems*. The Ecosystem Principle relates to the Law of Flow, which we said means that all living systems vascularize to form channels to accommodate flows. It also relates to the nature of the economy as being like a rainforest, as opposed to being like a thing that can be *built*, *run*, or *fixed*. The core idea is that the economy is not like a machine at all, but more akin to something biological—a complex adaptive system.

Machines can be complicated. Still, an individual can fully understand, design, and engineer their causes and effects. But no one can fully understand, design, and engineer an ecosystem. The same can be said for an advanced economy.

The implications of this principle are numerous, but the evolved nature of the economy stands out. Each organization functions analogously to an organism in a niche. The organism must consume enough calories to survive, whether large or small. The organization must earn enough revenue to survive, whether large or small. As other organisms compete in the evolutionary fitness landscape, any given organism must adapt. Would that it were so that an omnipotent, omniscient power could intercede to create better outcomes. There is no human equivalent to God, despite the posturing of the political class.

As we stand, mouths agape at the unfolding evolutionary ecosystem in which technological innovation functions, we will come to appreciate the failures almost as much as we do the successes. The ecosystemic view allows us to appreciate the feedback loops that continuously shape the living systems in which we will be able to flourish as human beings.

8. EMERGENCE

The extended economic order is a product of human actions, not human designs.

In comparing economies to evolutionary ecosystems, it is important to acknowledge that the Principle of Ecosystems has a twin: The Principle of Emergence. This principle states that the economy is a product of human actions, but not human designs. Continuing from the epigraph above, economist and philosopher F. A. Hayek writes:

> To the naive mind that can conceive of order only as the product of deliberate arrangement, it may seem absurd that in complex conditions order, and adaptation to the unknown, can be achieved more effectively by decentralizing decisions and that a division of authority will actually extend the possibility of overall order.[4]

From this insight, we might surmise that organizations, at least, can be designed and planned, but agree with Hayek that whole economies cannot. Hayek would have been enchanted by the new organizational forms made possible through new technology and new rules that lower transaction costs. It turns out that the Principle of Emergence can operate within organizations, too, and given the proper internal protocols, these organizations will become more and more competitive.

As with living systems, emergence in human systems means that complex phenomena arise from a set of simple rules. Just as cells in a body self-organize as organs thanks to a simpler set of nucleotides, people in an organization can self-organize into teams thanks to a simpler set of protocols.

9. TRANSACTION COSTS

Over time, entrepreneurial innovation is likely to reduce the costs of transacting and cooperating.

'Transaction' is a word that has associated taboos. But 'transaction costs' is a term of art in economics that refers to costs associated with value exchange. Because not all human relationships are direct exchanges—strictly speaking—we can extend the logic of transaction costs to cooperation.

Whether the parties immediately *get something* out of the interaction is not relevant to the question of how costly it is to interact. We can measure transaction costs in time, for example, *It took me a couple of hours to find you online.* We can measure transaction costs in opportunities foregone. *I could have been working on my book instead of waiting here in line.* Or we can measure transaction costs in monetary terms. *I had to pay a brokerage fee to find you.*

The essence of the idea—which helps to formulate a principle—is that those entrepreneurial innovations that lubricate cooperation should apply to any aspect of life where people stand to benefit from the interaction. That insight is perhaps no more apt than in the magisterium of governance. Yet today, our legacy systems too often *raise* cooperation costs. Whether in the top-down corporate form or in the corporate state, where these forms once reduced transaction costs, today they buckle under structural shortcomings as the world grows increasingly complex.

Institutional economics puts transaction costs squarely at the center of economic thinking, and so do we. In a certain sense, the Decentralist revolution is an effort to reduce transaction costs in areas where these costs might have been lower, historically, such as under various command and control systems. More importantly, though, new rules, new tools, and a new culture will change human power dynamics, in a way that allows more people to participate in the social, economic, and environmental life of the planet.

THERE IS no One True Way. That's why it is time to cross the governance paradigm with the economic paradigm to create markets *in governance*, which will replace markets *for governments* (corruption). Our ambitions are an affront to authoritarians and ideologues. No matter. As we create a new polycentric regime, we will do well to remember the Nine Principles of Markets. Because governance ought to be no different from any other good or service, the right mix of cooperation and competition is likely to improve customer outcomes. It may seem strange, but it is better to be a customer than a subject, or even a citizen. Why? Providers of governance services should compete in a global marketplace free of coercion. Poor performing governance organizations will die. And so they should.

The word 'customer' has a neutral or sometimes negative connotation. It can be associated either with the commercial domain in general or, specifically, with some sleazy car salesman who promises "great customer service." But when we consider the three major types of relationships between an individual and an organization, it should open our eyes.

- If you are a *subject*, the primary relationship is one of obedience.
- If you are a *citizen*, the primary relationship is acting in an illusion of consent, then obedience.

- If you are a *customer*, the primary relationship is one of consent.

The foregoing implies that the very idea of a public servant is largely a myth, and that it's time to change the connotation of 'customer.'

Citizens and subjects are an afterthought, whatever the stories we tell ourselves in civics class. If I am associated with a profit-seeking organization that renounces rent-seeking, I *must serve* those who choose to associate with me. If I am associated with a coercive state bureaucracy, I must serve a master with taxing authority (men with guns and jails).

These are fundamentally different relationships, and the preponderance of one or the other gives rise to the health or dysfunction of society. That's why a revolution in entrepreneurship—subversive innovation—is the tip of the spear for societal change. Never forget that you are launching your attack from the highest moral high ground of all: *consent*. Your enemies will have to fight you from the low perch of compulsion.

By applying the Nine Principles to the very idea of government, we will come to see that the Hobbesian idea of a single great power monopoly over some territory carries corrupting dynamics. The very idea of *One Ring to Rule Them All* will change utterly as soon as everyone gets a ring.

So, we have work to do.

10
MEANING: TEN KEYS

The tighter the connection with value, the greater the meaning.
- Robert Nozick, from *The Examined Life*[1]

"Why am I here?" a child asked his elder.
"For many reasons," said the elder.
"Such as?" she probed.
"So that we could have these talks," he said smiling.
The child was not satisfied.
"But what's the meaning of life?" she asked.
"The answer is troubling and promising," the elder replied. "But you must find the answer by living your life."
The child scratched her head then ran off to play.

MEANING MAKING

If meaning comes first from living one's life, one has to be in the world before there is any coherence to her story. But a child's natural inquisitiveness is a good match for the influx of experiences. After all, experience without inquiry is chaos. But in asking questions, we can begin to make sense out of the chaos. By answering such questions, one can begin to make meaning.

The elder's troubling and promising "answer" is that life has no meaning unless we contrive it. Then we must believe in the contrivance. This might strike you as a hollow formula at first blush. But it's powerful because some of our contrivances originate in our deepest recesses. Still, let us not get ahead of ourselves.

First, we must acknowledge that there is both an *individual* and *social* form of meaning-making. Both involve storytelling. In fact, despite centuries of philosophical hand-wringing, we have had the Keys to meaning in our grasp all along. If we are tempted to look for something more than these Keys, we risk straying into a wilderness of endless searching.

We began this journey to understanding by discussing the idea of happiness, which includes satisfying basic Maslovian needs, but extends into greater heights of being. Surely meaning lives in those heights. And meaning is inescapably subjective, which means it lies within the breast of the subject.

As I write in *After Collapse,*

> Meaning is a human construction. A derivation. A contrivance. Our socially constructed realities keep us from receding too quickly into the dark water. Still,

there is no meaning *in the world* waiting for us to discover it as one might a black hole, quark, or neutrino. Meaning doesn't live in the universe's fabric. The universe is a powerful self-referential loop. And it has questions.

Some will try to argue against the fact of subjectivity, but reality has other ideas. Apart from the human mirror of empathy, I cannot literally feel *your* joy or *your* pain. I can only feel my own. Meaning is the same. But that doesn't make the experience of meaning any less real. Continuing from *After Collapse*, I write:

> In our eagerness to share our meaning with others, perhaps to weave a shared reality, we invite others into solidarity. We weave our modes of meaning together intersubjectively. When we do so we're at our best. And we are not alone. But these filaments are so unique and so subtle, they have to be woven by each of us. Solidarity is intimate. It cannot be forced. It cannot be centralized. Any purported meaning that is forced or centralized is not meaning at all, but a uniform designed to make you lose yourself in the aspirations of the powerful. No. We must integrate our values with those of others, carefully, little by little, making room for transformation.

That being said, meaning can be inter-subjective. In other words, through narrative, we are not only capable of sharing some of who we are with one another, but we can also tell stories of who we are together.

As of this writing, we live in a time that seems decidedly bereft of meaning. And yet there is meaning to be made all around us. We need only to learn to tell the 'Story of Me' and the 'Story of Us.'

Let's begin with the Story of Me, in which the Ten Keys figure prominently. In the Story of Me, we appeal to a simple heuristic journalists once used. The ancients called it the *Septem Circumastiae*. Of the first six Keys, Rudyard Kipling wrote:

> *I keep six honest serving-men*
> *(They taught me all I knew);*
> *Their names are What and Why and When*
> *And How and Where and Who.*

1. CONTEXTUAL MEANING: WHAT?

The First Key is derived from one's functional role in a community. We call this *contextual meaning* because how he functions in context helps confer a piece of his identity. In ancient times, this was particularly important because everyone in the community had a vital role to play for every other person. *John is the blacksmith of our village. Charlotte is England's queen. Dwight is a Church deacon. Yoshi is a samurai in the Shogunate. Max is a father to three.* Meaning-making of this sort is mostly *external*, which is to say that others perceive him *as such and such* based on how he operates within the group. Today, contextual meaning can be a lot fuzzier because modernity is digitized, complex, and can move us into online simulacra of life. Still, one can rediscover this form of meaning simply by asking where he fits into the lives of those around him.

2. AUTHORED MEANING: WHO?

The Second Key is derived as one moves towards her Aspirational Self. We call this *authored meaning* because it is the kind of meaning that originates mostly from within. Authored meaning is perhaps the most Western of the Keys because it's the most individualistic. *I derive meaning from who I want to become.* During the Enlightenment, people began to understand themselves more as individuated selves. One could view her value as independent of her function within some collective. It's during this period we start to hear more rights talk, for example, such as that found in the work of Mary Wollstonecraft. The boxes of contextual meaning could no longer contain her genius. She spoke for others ready to develop, individuate, and author their lives, as the men had begun to do.

3. TELEOLOGICAL MEANING: WHY?

The Third Key is derived from the pursuit of a mission, tacit or explicit. We can call this *teleological meaning*. For example, if a physician is on a mission to cure a particular disease, she can find meaning in that pursuit. If she sets out on some mission with others, she might find a sense of place, which overlaps with contextual meaning. But with teleological meaning, the mission is a guide star that answers the *why* questions of her identity. *I have a sense of purpose.* It's common for someone without a purpose to feel hopeless, which implies that working towards a goal helps confer meaning. If one has a mission beyond the acquisition of status or possessions, one's effort towards that end helps justify her existence.

4. SITUATIONAL MEANING: WHERE?

The Fourth Key is derived from one's identification with others who share his values, are proximate, or who are at least culturally similar. We call this *situational meaning*. Because we rarely carry things out in isolation, we tend to bind together. Group identification offers a sense of place, which can come from our affiliations or nearness. This Key differs from contextual meaning in that situational meaning animates us in subtler ways. It's the ether of culture, defining one in ways that aren't so functional. It gives the Inuit multiple words for snow. It provides the Tar Heel with a taste for vinegar on pulled pork. It anneals one's brain so that he speaks with this accent or that. It's the fertile soil upon which cultural lives take root.

5. QUALITATIVE MEANING: HOW?

The Fifth Key is derived from striving for excellence in one's pursuits, roles, or personal development. We call this *qualitative meaning*. With this Key, one asks whether she is at her best or could be better. *Have you done your ten-thousand hours?* This question refers to putting in time for mastery. The *how* is not just the amount of effort she puts in, but how carefully and skillfully she worked. For example, the artist never makes the same art twice. She would probably find that labor tedious and fail to push the limits of her talents. Qualitative meaning thus involves one's refusal to settle for mediocrity in her craft.

6. TEMPORAL MEANING: WHEN?

The Sixth Key is derived from orienting ourselves in time. This orientation can be made relative to one's personal growth or epochal events of which we're all a part. We call this *temporal meaning* because it deals with our situation in time, history, and shared circumstances. People once found meaning in surviving the Great Depression or the Great Wars. Living in a connected age has meaning, too, just as we are at the genesis of the artificial intelligence age. This is meaning you and I share, but we cannot share that meaning with those who saw the stock market crash in 1929. And indeed there might be a disconnect between those who witnessed the Berlin Wall come down in 1989 and those born after that date who think Marxism is cool.

HUMANS ARE EVER-CHANGING loci of awareness within complex arrangements of atoms. We evolved the ability to regard ourselves and ask: Who? What? Why? Where? How? When? No one else can do that for us. No matter how strong, successful, or wise anyone else is, each makes her meaning, both alone and in collaboration. The Keys of Meaning are our unique vectors into which energy flows and becomes an identity. An endless source of wonder.

To the *Septem Circumstantiae*, for now, at least, let us say goodbye. There are other Keys to meaning that demand our exploration. Before we continue, remember that these prior six Keys are always a good place to start when it comes to meaning-making. You are invited, for example, to engage in a ritual that is available to you at most any time.

Place six pebbles in your hand (or you can use actual keys).

Imagine that each pebble represents a question. Answering these questions takes effort in reflection, but such effort can yield good fruit or perhaps help you discover something absent in the Story of You. When you think you have answered the questions enough to confer meaning, place the stones on the ground in a circle. Connect these answers in your mind in a fashion that forms a hexagram. The hexagram symbolizes something bigger than the sum of the parts, providing a clear basis for other Keys of Meaning that can help you unlock deeper mysteries.

7. DEVELOPMENTAL MEANING

The Seventh Key is derived from fundamental phase shifts in one's understanding or being. For example, when she ascends from the Order of the Pyramid to the Order of the Sun, she can find meaning in the transformation. Our lives present both obstacles and opportunities for growth. In developing as we do, it sometimes seems as if we see the world with fresh eyes. *Yes, now I see it. And I see it everywhere!* There is meaning in this, too. Not only is there meaning to be mined with the new set of cognitive or spiritual abilities, but there is also meaning to be made in the phase shift itself. There is meaning to be discovered outside the chrysalis and within the butterfly whose nature is forever changed.

8. WOVEN MEANING

The Eighth Key is derived from meaning-making with others. That is, there are some features of reality that are socially constructed and intersubjective. Woven meaning starts with what Metarelating expert Michael Porcelli calls "weaving shared reality."² Such is an exchange of communication in which two or more parties come to understand that there are "some things that are true for you and true for them, and you [all] know that's the case." Shared reality becomes meaningful in virtue of this process because other minds validate your perspective and you validate theirs. But more importantly, the woven reality takes on a life of its own that can animate a community. The promising aspect of woven meaning is a greater sense of solidarity around a set of ideas or values. The danger in woven meaning is that human beings sometimes try to weave a shared reality that ends up being directly at odds with the world around them, as a shared hallucination/psychosis or predatory cult. Healthy woven meaning requires us to take threads from a coherent understanding of reality, too.

9. NORMATIVE MEANING

The Ninth Key is derived from woven meaning, but meaning woven together with shared conceptions of the good. Philosophers will argue about whether moral entities are real, or if morality is just intersubjective agreement about certain kinds of sentiments. If the latter turns out to be true, that is enough. Moral systems take on greater importance the more people adhere to them. In Decentralism, we begin with the Six Spheres, which are timeless truths that we inherited from wise forebears. The more people who lock arms together around the Six Spheres, the more members will feel that they can trust the other members of their moral community. Trust is, after all, a happy byproduct of people who live more consistently within a moral universe together. Community members strive to maintain agreement about right and wrong, and that agreement helps bind the community together. And even though not everyone will share our priors or want to become part of our particular moral community, we are wise to live as examples to those others while maintaining a defensive posture. Because, as everyone knows, competition between incommensurable moral systems can quickly turn people into enemies.

10. TRANSCENDENT MEANING

The Tenth Key is derived from changes to *seeing* and *being* that one is certain of but that she cannot articulate. This form of meaning uses less *episteme* and more *gnosis*. The former means she relies on knowledge gained through the senses, while the latter means that she relies more on understanding gained through deep introspection. We have explored the idea of ineffable and the noetic, which is understanding one cannot describe in prose, and appears revelatory. Even though there is no magic in this kind of meaning, there is mystery. A sense of mystery, wonder, and sometimes love can flood every cell in one's body. Experiences of *transcendent meaning* can be ephemeral. Other times they can leave a residue. But it is in their rarity and the corresponding sense of apprehending something so true, beautiful, and good that one cannot help but submit to its meaningfulness. Try reducing the meaning of a parent's love to biology. Only a non-parent would even try. Transcendent meaning can include symbolic or mythic forms of meaning, conveying more than the merely prosaic. Transcendent meaning might be troubling to the perceptive acolyte concerned that this dimension works at odds with Rationality. After all, transcendent meaning arrives via means that seem to militate against reason and evidence. Master practitioners will discover that Rationality and transcendent meaning can be consilient.

THE STORY OF US

When a civilization loses its story, the people soon lose their civilization. Relativism and postmodernism have prompted so many to question their own stories. In fact, at one stage in the history of thought, it became fashionable to challenge all metanarratives. But in so doing, the challengers never bothered to offer any structural replacements. The people have, in some sense, lost their scaffolding *as a people*. The result has been cultural disorientation, which has created a lost generation. We can become unmoored, adrift, lost in a sea of sorrow. What the Order of the Nautilus and the Order of the Lotus have to teach us is that we must reclaim our metanarratives. Or better, we must tell new stories. We need new stories in which we can track the truth, grow as individuals, and cooperate more at scale.

Because there can be no gatekeepers to civilization-defining stories, we have to get better at meaning-making, particularly woven meaning and normative meaning. Prior to that, we have to start by looking for that which seems absent in all of us.

It used to be that a people was tied to some territory, and their story written on a certain patch of earth. History is thus littered with tales of angry apes killing each other over these patches. But decentralization means that more and more people can connect in the cloud, which means it is possible to find solidarity in stories we share with people far away. Unfortunately, people will coalesce around different metanarratives that will surely clash.

Must there be an even greater story, then? Jews tell the story of their people's escaping Pharaoh, but they invite strangers to sit at the table with them to share in the closeness and blessings of liberation. Christians tell the story of God's son who came to earth in the form of a man so that he could die for all of us and provide us a path to salvation. Muslims tell of a great prophet who is the final prophet, and his words united warring tribes under *tawhid*, the 'assertion of absolute oneness.' Buddhists relate the story of the Siddartha Gautama who tried first to become an ascetic but learned that Nirvana, 'the blowing out,' cannot be achieved through suffering. One must achieve Nirvana through freeing oneself from desire, which is the source of suffering. And not all Great Stories are religious. There are secular stories too. The American Revolution and Founding blend history with mythic meaning around liberal ideals, which has managed to transcend and include the religious stories that bind the faithful in America. But that story is being dissolved.

Where does that leave us? And who is "us"? We are the Decentralists. We are a small group that barely has a story. Our story is nascent and continues to be written—but soon by the many. Like a lowly scribe toiling away in the tower, I set out to write this document knowing full well that I am but a curator of concepts that span multiple generations and multiple dimensions of life. And my hope is that, just like the developers who have organized around seminal documents and unleashed new systems of economic value, people will organize around works like this to unleash new communities of interpretation, morality, and meaning.

More and more people are locking arms around Decentralism, as inchoate as it has been up to this point. Some outlines are emerging. Others are vague, like our hope that technology and agency can help to bring out the best in us while liberating us from the predators and ideologues who currently run the world; others are clear and stark, like the logic of a smart contract. All are vital to our evolving story.

MEANING: TEN KEYS

IN 2009, a mysterious figure or group of figures named Satoshi Nakamoto assembled knowledge from some of the most brilliant minds on earth. He distilled that knowledge into specifications for a holistic system, a nine-page document that is a kind of foundational scripture.[3] Satoshi is a major prophet in a succession of minor Decentralist prophets, but his prophecy was delivered in code. The prophecy was always about more than profit. Satoshi showed the way through the Red Sea of government debt and dysfunction, into the moral universe of collaboration and community.

The bitcoin white paper had only a few technical specs from which one could make any number of inferences. A hive of developers would make quite important interpretations in code—where a new fork would represent a new body of interpretations. Some variations would drive communities to divide into new sects, which would create their own competing forks. As with the Hebrew Talmud, these forks required people to engage in *rational discourse such that these systems could be executed or exited.*

Satoshi Nakamoto's Interpreters were not just those who would create sectarian forks. Others launched entire new networks with unique features, properties, and limitations beyond bitcoin. Still, the aggregate is an ecosystem of systems experiencing a Cambrian explosion. Thus, from that original paper, Satoshi Nakamoto was able to catalyze an entire ecosystem of minds who could instantiate a set of ideas and maintain them, but without any controlling authority.

Still, various interpreters of Satoshi's genius vied for dominance. Incredibly, people are uniting in a proto-doctrine: Decentralism. It's time we gave it more contours and a name. Beyond the technical specifications of Bitcoin, many features of that proto-doctrine appear in this volume, which is an effort to bring greater clarity to Decentralism. To do so will allow the doctrine to transition away from its pupal stage, that is, to spread its wings and fly in the minds of the many.

In this transition, we can learn to self-govern and therefore thrive within systems of trust, mutual support, and mutual benefit. Not only will we learn frugality again as cryptocurrencies change our time preferences, we will also become more cosmopolitan as we connect to those who share our perspective, which is a perspective beyond race, ethnicity, and nationality.

We also understand that decentralization is not an end state but instead is a continuously churning series of efforts by real people—sometimes in competition, other times in collaboration—coming together in a greater orbit of possibility.

Decentralism transforms humanity. Instead of a few powerful people making decisions on behalf of the many through threats, appropriation, or trickery, true self-government is within our grasp. When Alexis de Tocqueville came to America, he observed a people engaged in the "art of association":

> When citizens can associate only in certain cases, they regard association as a rare and singular process, and they hardly think of it.
>
> When you allow them to associate freely in everything, they end up seeing in association the universal and, so to speak, unique means that men can use to attain the various ends that they propose. Each new need immediately awakens the idea of association. The art of association then becomes, as I said above, the mother science; everyone studies it and applies it.[4]

Decentralism's innovations extend the art of association beyond the geographically proximate. And of course, cryptocurrencies let people hold different forms of property that will become more and more difficult to take by force. Likewise, Decentralism empowers people to participate in different forms of organization, and participatory power becomes harder to usurp.

The impetus to threaten violence against another is often driven by a desire to take possession of others' resources, or to control them in some way. But decentralization tends to make such impulses more costly. And when the cost of oppression, appropriation, or usurpation goes up, the cost of peace, freedom, and abundance goes down.

If Decentralism is a doctrine that includes the Six Spheres, Decentralists will continue to practice the Spheres, or find ways to instantiate them in code. We believe the Six Spheres should extend to every aspect of our lives, and the degree to which they do is the degree to which we will enjoy flourishing on our various forking paths. After all, there are sources of meaning along every path. It is up to each of us to shape our lives through practice, and to derive meaning from reflecting on that process. Over and over.

Meaning's Ten Keys should not be stored away somewhere to collect dust. Instead, we should use them to unlock doorways of possibility, transformation, and change. The Story of You and the Story of Us are waiting to be written. And those stories will inspire future generations to follow a path of peace, freedom, and abundance over one of domination, and destitution.

MANICHAEISM: AN AFTERWORD

Truth is one; sages call it by various names.

- from, *The Rig Veda*

When most people hear the term Manichaean, they usually think about black and white thinking as opposed to a dualistic religion from Mesopotamia. Whether they're more enlightened or more sanctimonious, those who use the term are almost always pointing out another's apparent inability to see that the world is full of shades. It's fashionable again to speak in Hegelian terms about a given issue—*thesis, antithesis,* and *synthesis.*

In many circumstances, this is a good and healthy practice. Synthesist thinking requires you to try on, as it were, different perspectives before settling on one. Or better, perhaps, you find a reasoned middle ground that integrates partial truths of extreme views. Life is complicated. People can operate in good faith and still have different perspectives. And, indeed, the practice of *pluralism*—one of the Six Spheres—requires us to look for facets of truth in all the perspectives before collapsing into a single perspective that might be missing important insights.

Yet, I would like to argue that there is room for Manichaean thinking in our postmodern world. In other words, there are certain domains in which we must be fairly uncompromising in our commitments. We have to be Manichae-ish. If Manichaeish has never been a word before, it is now. Because, by Manichaeish, we must act like Mani in a couple of important ways.

First, like Mani, we have to be *universalist*. That means some moral practices should apply in every domain of life and at every scale. The Six Spheres are one such set of practices. Even if they are not moral laws we can discover through moral reasoning, we should always endeavor to practice them. And we are not alone in this assessment. The Vedantic traditions all adhere to the idea of universal practices, even if individual adherents routinely fall short. We are human, or what the Christians call fallen. At the end of the day, we seek to form a moral community whose members share our priorities.

Second, like Mani, we have to be *missionaries*. That doesn't mean we have to act like crazy people who knock on doors or estrange ourselves from our friends and family in the service of Decentralism. Quite the opposite. If we want more people who radiate peace like monks meditating in the forest, we have first to practice daily and then patiently share our gnosis. After all, one of the Seven Rituals is outreach. The form of outreach you employ should play to your communication and practitioner strengths. Implicit in being a missionary is finding courage and resolve. It is not about manipulation, selling fear, finding fault, or badgering anyone. These are bludgeons. Outreach is first being a good example and then sharing knowledge in the appropriate life contexts.

Remember that, at its core, Manichaeism was also a synthesist doctrine. After all, Mani and his followers integrated the wisdom and prophets of prior traditions, including both Jesus and the Buddha, into a single, canonical worldview that Mani set out before he died. At its root, Manichaeism was a type of Gnosticism. And like Gnosticism, Decentralism offers humanity a better world through special knowledge (*gnosis*). As with Manichaeism, we have sometimes to evaluate the world in starker binaries. Put another way, we apply principles. So, dualities such as *nonviolence* or *violence*, *integrity* or *corruption*, and *stewardship* or *negligence* become facets of *good* or *evil*. So we must become more comfortable talking about good and evil again.

Now, it might seem strange to maintain that we have to be both Manichaeish on the one hand and synthesist on the other, but we do. These are not contradictory positions. The universals of Decentralism are no good as abstractions. We must practice them daily. That is, truly to reap the benefit of their guidance, we must make them meaningful. And to make them meaningful, we must make them real to us. Making them real to us is transmutation through active practice. And in praxis, we will see the good radiate outward from our being, then radiated back to us from others. When we combine such radiant beings into an ever-expanding moral community, the human condition will steadily improve. We can be as monks. The world is our meditation forest. Our liberation from Centralism might be as close as we will ever get to salvation.

Decentralism includes similarities to Manichaeism in that there is an opposing force, a dark side. We have called it Centralism and, occasionally, the Church of State. To understand why it lies in opposition, we must return to the Six Spheres and the Six Offenses once more:

Violence. Centralism is the religion of politics, which, as we have suggested, is an entire magisterium built upon the threat of violence. We have built Decentralism upon a foundation of nonviolence. In Manichaeish terms, persuasion is the path of light. Compulsion is the path of darkness.

Corruption. To win in the Centralist matrix, one has almost always to auction off his integrity. There are simply fewer people at the highest echelons of central power. So competitors have to be eliminated. The means for eliminating competitors straddle either side of legal lines and trample over moral ones. There are, of course, differences of both degree and kind when it comes to corruption and some authorities are more corrupt than others. Our concept of corruption is Manichaeish enough to include any machinations that enrich the political actor or expand his influence through illiberal means. But the Ring is always there, tempting the powerful with the bounties of a great negative-sum game. And this game selects for sociopaths.

Callousness. Centralism also beckons us to turn away from *compassion*. Those who want to seem compassionate will shroud themselves in a kind of illusion. Not only are they callous to those who object to the state's threats of violence and expropriation, they see political means as a stand-in for charitable acts. In other words, voting for some platform or program is not really compassion. Outsourcing one's compassion is a way to signal rectitude. Under our conception, one should give away everything she owns before she even thinks of obliging people with guns to confiscate another's property. Compulsion is not compassion.

Monomania. Centralism is the religion of the One True Way. Bureaucrats, activists, and partisans labor under the notion that there must be no divergent paths from the law, much less from executive orders issued by our modern Emperors. *Pluralism* is not just an acknowledgment that different people have different conceptions of the good. Pluralism requires active practice, which includes integrating different truths and tolerating other ways of living, as long as those divergent ways are products of consent. Monomania is baked into Centralism because it is the nature of central authority to impose conformity and constrain diversity.

Negligence. Centralists imagine that the state is somehow a good and rightful steward of resources. Yet the list of resources the state wastes or neglects constitutes a book unto itself. Governments routinely incur debts greater than their gross domestic products (GDP). Governments pay exorbitant sums to contractors that no market would bear. State-managed forests fare poorly compared to privately managed forests. The United States government is the world's largest polluter by far, and its military pollutes more than 100 countries.[1] State-managed roads fall into disrepair as new roads are being constructed in a Congressman's wilderness. Social security coffers are bare. Centralist systems create incentives for negligence, and the political class is shaped by those incentives no matter how much they posture and peacock on the campaign trail. Those who follow them do so in negligence, not stewardship, so we won't call them sheep. Even sheep do the work of grazing.

Casuistry. Politics hones the art of casuistry, and politics is the Centralist's home. So when you hear promises that sound too good to be true, or hear an appointee baffle the fawning press with bullshit, you know you're in the Church of State. Casuistry is not just the highest value of the political class, power's handmaidens – whether the media or the activists – learn to recite talking points as part of Centralist liturgy. When rationality gets reduced to rhetoric, truth is the first casualty.

Now, if you doubt that Centralism engenders the Six Offenses, consider some of the world's natural experiments: Germany and Korea, specifically when both countries were split, East and West, North and South, respectively. None of these is a perfect exemplar of Decentralist or Centralist institutions, but they are good enough for comparisons, especially in a time before the Internet. In *The Social Singularity,* I relate the following, which deserves a lengthy quote:

> A group of behavioral economists wanted to study the difference between cultural values after years in different institutional settings. Specifically, the team of Lars Hornuf of the University of Munich, and Dan Ariely, Ximena García-Rada, and Heather Mann of Duke University ran a test to determine Germans' willingness to lie for personal gain. Some 250 Berliners (the citizens, not the doughnuts) were randomly selected to take part in a game where they could win up to $8.00. And the game involved opportunities to gain through lying and cheating.[2]
>
> According to *The Economist,* after wrapping up the game, the players had to fill out a form that "asked their age and the part of Germany where they had lived in different decades." The researchers concluded that, on average, those participants with East German roots cheated twice as much as those who had grown up in West Germany. The team also looked at how much time the participants had spent in either place prior to the fall of the Berlin Wall. "The longer the participants had been exposed to socialism, the greater the

likelihood that they would claim improbable numbers of high rolls."[3]

Why did these two groups perform so differently?

The study did not prove the causal determinants of the different behaviors. But we can speculate. First, we can safely rule out the hypothesis that East Germans are born with a predilection to cheat and lie. Both sets come from more or less the same genetic stock. It's also doubtful that the differences in moral outlook came from differences in, say, diet. So the likeliest explanation for the difference is that the two vastly different sets of rules eventually shaped the values of the peoples.

We become what we follow. We shape our rules and then our rules shape us.[4]

In this book, I have endeavored to show that we are not just passive victims of our institutions. We have agency. We have morality. We have culture. And we have meaning to make. Just as East Germans risked death to scale the wall or tunnel beneath it, we can find courage in our will to liberate ourselves and others. Just as Yeonmi Park found her way out of North Korea after years of abuse and neglect, today she lives in relative freedom. Still, she watches in horror as darkness descends over civilization as Centralism ascends.

The darkness flows not from any external threat but from within the human heart. We are beings capable of happiness and flourishing, but sometimes we push our fears and anxieties into the shadows. There they fester. And from those deep psychological bowers, fear, and anxiety reemerge transformed.

To live right now, then, is to live in paradox. Despite

conditions of relative peace and abundance, a psychosocial pathology has taken hold. It manifests itself as something like a replacement religion. Where people once turned to their temples and communities for reassurance, more turn now to political authority. Merchants of fear magnify the significance of certain human problems, which obscures complicated truths and feeds the dogmas of this new faith, whose adherents characterize Decentralists as evil. Adherents to Centralism believe they are on the side of the angels, but their faith threatens to bring about a Dark Age. Why? Because more and more people in the grip of this religion are willing to use the fist.

UPGRADING FROM DOS

We have been living in DOS (democratic operating system) for so long it's hard for most people to imagine anything other than the Red App and the Blue App. Or, to mix metaphors, we see Team Blue on one end of the rope and Team Red on the other. Then we're told to pick a team to see which side gets dragged through the mud. Fail to play this game and you're shirking your duty: *If you don't vote you have no right to complain,* they'll say.

Americans have been fattened on a steady diet of civic lore about democracy, but that system now locks partisans in perpetual warfare. Each 'side' holds out hope that one day, they'll get to shove their One True Way down the others' throats. But Decentralists see things very differently.

Though sentimental attachment to voting and elections seems indomitable, a few are beginning to understand new ways to organize. It's true that day by day our civic consciousness is being replaced by animus. So it rarely occurs to anyone that there could be another way.

I'd like to make the case that the only way to win is to play a different game.

To live in the world as a Decentralist is to struggle against the fact of power. But that struggle should sound familiar. What Decentralists insist upon is what the American Founders promised, which is that we the governed, must give our *consent*. This is a moral-political principle that is absolutely antithetical to Centralism.

We make no determinations about the mode and manner of governance. The rulesets we choose could be like those of the Israeli kibbutz or the Kyoto Prefecture. The key is having the choice. Making such choices means moving, inch by inch, towards a decentralized, consent-based order.

THE ONE TRUE WAY

Authoritarianism is on the rise. More and more people think that society can and ought to be ordered administratively. All it takes to fix a social issue or help some group is to pass a law, fund a program, and grow a bureaucracy. The left/right distinction matters less.

Each 'side' doubles down on illiberal, social control measures whenever it suits them. The left has cast its lot with identity politics, which includes moralistic crusades, crocodile tears, and shaming mobs. The right has become merely reactionary, pushed along by crude nationalism, imperial military aspirations, or nostalgia for a time that never was. Occasionally, bizarrely, they'll switch positions as is politically expedient. Both sides seem willing to discard the idea that freedom and free inquiry light our world. And neither side seems interested in addressing the brute fact that, for example, the U.S. federal debt stands at 135 percent of GDP as of this writing. Such is life under the Church of State.

Because each side fancies theirs is the One True Way they leave no room for other perspectives, much less other ways of organizing society. Their titanic warfare has become an ongoing spectacle, which distracts the rest of us from the promise of humane cooperation within a liberal, pluralistic order. So, it is time for us to fulfill that promise before it can no longer be fulfilled. And this will take courage.

A DIFFERENT GAME

Given such enormous power, how are we to play a different game?

Political scientist James C. Scott reminds us that more "regimes have been brought, piecemeal, to their knees by what was once called "Irish democracy," the silent, dogged resistance, withdrawal, and truculence of millions of ordinary people, than by revolutionary vanguards or rioting mobs."

So first, we have to adopt that mien of silent, dogged resistance. Wherever possible, we have to drag our feet, refuse to comply, and make the costs of enforcement too high for authorities.

Then, we have to practice *satyagraha*. This Sanskrit word means roughly "truth force," and Mahatma Gandhi taught his followers to use *satyagraha* against the British Raj. The Freedom Riders and Civil Rights activists used similar tactics in the Jim Crow South. *Satyagraha* is thus a nonviolent means, even as it exerts enormous pressure against powerful hierarchies.

Today we possess technological tools that Gandhi or MLK could scarcely have imagined. So in practicing *satyagraha*, we must do so through the best available means—lateralization—coordinating both asynchronously and in real-time. Such includes discovering new opportunities for exit. But I'm not just talking about voting with your feet, though that can be a fruitful approach. I'm also talking about 'voting' with your money, which includes voting for new money. I'm talking about *entering* new systems, too, the net effect of which will be the creation of new markets in governance.

EXIT STRATEGIES

Let's get into some examples of exit, which can be understood as an extension of *satyagraha*.

1. *Adopt cryptocurrencies.* These are not just digital money. They represent a thousand alternatives to institutional middlemen, including the state, which is the greatest middleman of all. Go deep into the token universe. There you will discover a wonderland of possibilities in parallel governance. From distributed autonomous organizations (DAOs) to smart contracts and decentralized finance, the technology's growth has gone exponential.
2. *Move to a different state or country.* You probably realize that one of the freest states in the U.S. is New Hampshire. But did you know that one of the freest places in the world is on the island of Roatan, Honduras? Prospera, a new governance project, boasts an uncorrupted common-law system and ultra-low taxes. Going abroad might not be for you. But it's important to remember that staying put is a kind of voting, too.
3. *Migrate away from Big Tech.* The dominant search engine manipulates its results according to narrow doxa. Maybe it's time to try Presearch. The

dominant video hosting service censors its talent and plays handmaiden to authorities. Maybe it's time to try Odysee. The dominant social media platforms routinely remove accounts of those brave enough to challenge institutional narratives—and they own all your data. Stay tuned then for the rollout of decentralized social media apps such as Junto.
4. *Take your children out of the government school system.* The pandemic has sent parents and students scurrying to alternatives such as The Socratic Experience, Acton Academy, or Thales Academy. Many are realizing these alternatives are not just better than Centralist schools, but affordable, despite more of our tax dollars being siphoned into a system that never seems to improve, controlled not by parents but by partisan unions and identitarians.
5. *Support only higher education institutions that embrace liberalism.* It's no secret that most colleges have become illiberal indoctrination camps. But not all of them. One of the most interesting colleges in the world is Universidad Francisco Marroquin (UFM) in Guatemala. UFM teaches entrepreneurship and the professors are themselves entrepreneurial. Whatever college you support, it's important to remove any distorting lenses that cause you to see sports teams or nostalgia. These keep you from seeing the rot behind the veneer of legacy prestige. We must also remember that knowledge is not schooling, and education is not a plaque. It might well be time to exit the guild-cartel of higher education entirely and never look back.

6. *Form strong, local separatist movements.* The United States was formed thanks to a separatist movement. Now its federal authority has grown like a cancer on the backs of the people, just as the Anti-Federalists warned that it would. Let us combine the spirit of 1776 with satyagraha. And in that spirit, we must come to terms with the idea that the Union, such as it is, is no longer worth preserving. It's time for conscientious people everywhere to fight for self-determination. Join or start your own separatist movement, even if that movement lives in the digital cloud.
7. *Practice tax avoidance.* It's completely legal to avoid taxes. In fact, it's hard to find anyone who doesn't. The key is to do it well. That means walking right up to legal barriers to keep as much of your earnings as you can. Tax avoidance strategies include offshoring your wealth and using pretax vehicles. There are really smart advisors out there to help.
8. *Start or join a mutual aid organization.* Benefit societies and mutual aid organizations seem like a thing of the past. But people trapped in the idea that the entitlement system is going to be there for them in a decade or so should think again. Despite the hefty sums we're forced to contribute to near-insolvent systems like Social Security and Medicare, we need to start building our own backup plans. Mutual aid systems create community as members apply local knowledge and direct governance.
9. *Start up a self-managed organization.* Gandhi is credited with saying *Be the change you want to see in the world.* Management philosophies like Morning

Star self-management and Holacracy offer companies to run on rules without rulers. Every new company operating this way is a data point demonstrating that a world without a managerial class is not only possible but desirable.

The above list is certainly not exhaustive. I offer these examples with the hope that they will catalyze a commitment to what writer Michael P. Gibson calls underthrow. Gibson thinks underthrow will lead to a pluralistic market in governance.

"All laws must be strictly opt-in. Lawmakers could be saints, devils or monkeys on typewriters—it doesn't matter. The opt-out/opt-in system lets only good laws survive. Bad laws are driven out of production."[5]

Such is the consent of the governed. And it is how one takes steps towards decentralization. Whether humanity ever arrives at the Consensual Society is another question altogether, but one that depends on you and me.

MENTIONS

With this book, I draw from the wisdom of ages, and a great intellectual commons. Most importantly, I draw from intimate conversations with friends and loved ones.

The Decentralist is designed to be a manifesto for an emerging doctrine. Regardless of this book's direct impact, my hope is that the principles of Decentralism spread far and wide. If my role as scribe brings this doctrine into greater focus, I will have left a meaningful trace. I couldn't have done it without a little help from my friends.

Deep appreciation goes to my mentor Chris Rufer whose name has appeared in every book I've ever published. There's a reason for that. I cherish his influence and all the support he has given me in my career.

Thanks to James Harrigan for his deepening friendship and role as editor. His willingness to call bullshit, cry uncle, offer praise, and flag bad sentences has helped me craft a better book. James is also proof that grown men can become great friends.

Enormous gratitude goes to Rich Dalton for his valuable and thoughtful copyediting.

Michael Porcelli and I have made intellectual rapport a permanent fixture of our friendship. Many of those conversations appear on the Social Evolution podcast, which I hope enjoys a long life in the eager ears of an ever-expanding audience.

Love and thanks go to Jennifer Clary for her work in formatting and typesetting. This is her second foray into such an effort. She also happens to be the wonderful mother of our daughter Sophia.

I am lucky that I get to engage with brilliant people who teach me, including Tarun Nimmagadda, Matt Gilliland, David Fuller, Luke Nosek, John Hagel III, Michel Bauwens, Jim Rutt, Brian Robertson, Eric Alston, and Justin Arman. (Writing this book was Justin's idea.)

Elizabeth Hunker and Jake Vartanian have provided excellent guidance on integrating my work with non-fungible tokens. Their continued effort in the cryptocurrency space is a spear tip.

Moral support from Jenny Clary, James Harrigan, Shannon Ewing, and Tyler Bel has been invaluable.

My deep veneration goes to Paul Walker, who raised me to become a good father, a music lover, and a spiritual seeker. Patricia Hord-Heatherley proved to me that love transcends categories like blood, which she demonstrates by simply radiating it. My mother, Ann Hord-Heatherley, will always be my hero and my rock. My aunt, Jean Roberts, always believed in me. My late father, Rick Borders, still speaks to me with foul-mouthed brilliance and a clumsy affection. His wife Patsy continues to shine as an example of faith and compassion.

My daughter Sophia teaches me to have a strong will and a good heart. My son Felix teaches me to give of oneself lovingly and without conditions. My son Sid teaches me that the life of non-conformity and commitment to what's right, though a difficult road, is a road worth taking.

—END

NOTES

MOTIVATION: AN INTRODUCTION

1. Borges, Jorges Luis. In *The Garden of Forking Paths*. Penguin Classics, 2018.
2. See also "the Experience Machine" from Robert Nozick's *Philosophical Explanations*.

1. MISSION: ONE REVOLUTION

1. Timothy C. May. "The Crypto Anarchist Manifesto." Accessed March 13, 2022. https://www.activism.net/cypherpunk/crypto-anarchy.html.
2. Lysander Spooner. *No Treason: The Constitution of No Authority*. Fpp Classics, 2015.
3. Michael P. Gibson. "The Nakamoto Consensus — How We End Bad Governance - Michael P Gibson." *Medium*, April 3, 2015. https://medium.com/@William_Blake/the-nakamoto-consensus-how-we-end-bad-governance-2d75b2fa1f65.
4. Paul-Emile de Puydt. "Panarchy (1860)" Accessed March 13, 2022. https://www.panarchy.org/depuydt/1860.eng.html.
5. Jackie Mansky. "Eight Secret Societies You Might Not Know." *Smithsonian Magazine*, March 7, 2016. https://www.smithsonianmag.com/history/secret-societies-you-might-not-know-180958294/.
6. Confusingly, the Antifederalists were more 'federalist' than the Federalists, in that they believed in a higher degree of power devolution.
7. Satoshi Nakamoto. "Bitcoin: A Peer-to-Peer Electronic Cash System" https://bitcoin.org/bitcoin.pdf.
8. Michael C. Munger. *Regulation*. "The ThingI The Thing Itself" Accessed March 13, 2022. https://www.cato.org/sites/cato.org/files/serials/files/regulation/1999/10/reviews.pdf.
9. P2P Foundation. "Commoning." Accessed March 13, 2022. http://wiki.p2pfoundation.net/Commoning.
10. Max Borders. "How We Become the Social Safety Net - Social Evolution - Medium." *Social Evolution*, July 17, 2018. https://medium.com/social-evolution/how-we-become-the-social-safety-net-2994a68a53db.

2. MEANS: TWO HANDS

1. Antony Davies and James Harrigan. *Cooperation & Coercion: How Busybodies Became Busybullies and What That Means for Economics and Politics*. Open Road Media, 2020.
2. "Wushu Greeting." Accessed March 13, 2022. https://www.jocasta.me/TaiChi/Classes/greeting.html.

3. MIND: THREE GOVERNORS

1. Gardiner Morse. "Decisions and Desire." Harvard Business Review, January 1, 2006. https://hbr.org/2006/01/decisions-and-desire.

4. MATRIX: FOUR FORCES

1. Frank Herbert. *Dune*. Penguin, 2005.
2. Sigmund Freud. "Beyond the Pleasure Principle." In *Beyond the Pleasure Principle*., 1–83. London: The International Psycho-Analytical Press. Accessed March 14, 2022. http://dx.doi.org/10.1037/11189-001.
3. Adrian Bejan and Sylvie Lorente. "The Constructal Law of Design and Evolution in Nature." *Philosophical Transactions of the Royal Society of London. Series B, Biological Sciences* 365, no. 1545 (May 12, 2010): 1335–47. https://doi.org/10.1098/rstb.2009.0302.
4. Etymology, origin and meaning of aspire by etymonline. "Definition and Etymology of Aspire." Accessed March 14, 2022. https://www.etymonline.com/word/aspire.

5. MUTUALITY: FIVE DISRUPTIONS

1. Daniel C. Dennett. *Darwin's Dangerous Idea: Evolution and the Meaning of Life*. Simon and Schuster, 2014.
2. Justin Goro. "The Great Hard Fork: An Unraveling of State Legitimacy." *Social Evolution*, January 18, 2018. https://medium.com/social-evolution/the-great-hard-fork-an-unraveling-of-state-legitimacy-a559b7d125ed.
3. Nathaniel Scharping. "The Lost World of the Maya Is Finally Emerging From the Jungle." *Discover Magazine*, February 7, 2019. https://www.discovermagazine.com/planet-earth/the-lost-world-of-the-maya-is-finally-emerging-from-the-jungle.
4. Dwight D Eisenhower. "Military Industrial Complex Speech." n.d. https://www.militaryindustrialcomplex.com/military-industrial-complex-speech.php.

5. Anthony Capaccio. "Pentagon Contractor's 9,400% Profit on Half-Inch Pin Challenged." *Bloomberg Quint*, May 15, 2019. https://www.bloombergquint.com/business/pentagon-contractor-s-9-400-profit-on-half-inch-pin-challenged.

6. MORALITY: SIX SPHERES

1. Swami Satchidananda. *The Yoga Sutras of Patanjali*. Integral Yoga Dist, 2012.
2. The following is excerpted and adapted from *After Collapse*.
3. Thich Nhat Hanh. *Living Buddha, Living Christ: 20th Anniversary Edition*. Penguin, 2007.
4. Ibid.
5. Swami Mukundananda. "Chapter 7, Verse 2 – Bhagavad Gita, The Song of God" *Bhagavad Gita*. Accessed March 14, 2022. https://www.holy-bhagavad-gita.org/chapter/7/verse/2.
6. Robert Nozick. *Philosophical Explanations*. Harvard University Press, 1981.

7. MINDFULNESS: SEVEN RITUALS

1. Viktor Frankl. *Man's Search for Meaning*. Beacon Press, 2006.
2. Eliza Barclay. "A Buddhist Monk Explains Mindfulness for Times of Conflict." *Vox*, November 22, 2016. https://www.vox.com/science-and-health/2016/11/22/13638374/buddhist-monk-mindfulness.
3. Joseph Campbell. "Joseph Campbell: 'A Ritual Is the Enactment of a Myth. And, by Participating in the Ritual, You Are Participating in the Myth....'" Joseph Campbell Foundation, January 15, 2019. https://www.jcf.org/works/quote/ritual-is-the-enactment/.

8. MATURATION: EIGHT STAGES

1. Genesis 28: 10-19. O. T. English. 1985. *Tanakh*. Philadelphia: Jewish Publication Society, 1985.
2. Clare W Graves. *The Never Ending Quest: Clare W. Graves Explores Human Nature*, 2005.
3. I draw heavily from the work of Clare Graves (original), Don Beck and Christopher Cowen (Spiral Dynamics), and Ken Wilber (Integral Theory).

9. MARKETS: NINE PRINCIPLES

1. Alex Tabarrok. "A Price Is a Signal Wrapped Up in an Incentive," February 14, 2017. https://marginalrevolution.com/marginalrevolution/2017/02/price-signal-wrapped-incentive.html.
2. Political entrepreneurs prefer to extract monopoly rents through collusion with authorities. (An economic rent is any benefit to a producer in excess of the costs needed to bring a good or service into production. Rent-seekers normally extract rents by colluding with authorities or taking advantage of state transfers.)
3. Michael Strong. "An Introduction to Strong's Law." *Radical Social Entrepreneurs*. Accessed March 14, 2022. https://www.radicalsocialentreps.org/2017/11/an-introduction-to-strongs-law/.
4. F. A. Hayek. *The Fatal Conceit: The Errors of Socialism*. Routledge, 2013.

10. MEANING: TEN KEYS

1. Nozick, Robert. *Examined Life: Philosophical Meditations*. Simon and Schuster, 1990. 168.
2. Michael Porcelli. "Weaving Shared Reality — Michael Porcelli." *Michael Porcelli*, March 13, 2020. https://www.themichaelporcelli.com/writing/2020/3/12/weaving-shared-reality.
3. Satoshi Nakamoto. "Bitcoin: A Peer-to-Peer Electronic Cash System" https://bitcoin.org/bitcoin.pdf.
4. Alexis de Tocqueville. *Democracy in America*. Signet Classics, 2001.

MANICHAEISM: AN AFTERWORD

1. Benjamin Neimark, Oliver Belcher, and Patrick Bigger. "US Military Is a Bigger Polluter than 140 Countries Combined." *Quartz*, June 28, 2019. https://qz.com/1655268/us-military-is-a-bigger-polluter-than-140-countries-combined/.
2. The Economist. "Lying Commies." *The Economist*, July 19, 2014. https://www.economist.com/news/finance-and-economics/21607830-more-people-are-exposed-socialism-worse-they-behave-lying-commies.
3. ibid.
4. Max Borders. *After Collapse: The End of America and the Rebirth of Her Ideals*. Social Evolution, 2021.
5. Michael P. Gibson. "The Nakamoto Consensus — How We End Bad Governance" *Medium*, April 3, 2015. https://medium.com/@William_Blake/the-nakamoto-consensus-how-we-end-bad-governance-2d75b2fa1f65.

Made in the USA
Columbia, SC
28 June 2022

62377948R00117